20 Guided Meditations For Deep Sleep & Anxiety (2 in 1): Positive Affirmations & Hypnosis For Raising Your Vibration, Self-Love, Relaxation, Overthinking, Insomnia & Depression

Guided Meditations For Deep Sleep: 10 Hours Of Positive Affirmations, Hypnosis& Breathwork- Relaxation, Self-Love & Overcoming Anxiety, Overthinking, Insomnia& Depression

By Self-healing Mindfulness Academy

© Copyright 2021 - All rights reserved.

The content contained within this book may not be reproduced, duplicated or transmitted without direct written permission from the author or the publisher.
Under no circumstances will any blame or legal responsibility be held against the publisher, or author, for any damages, reparation, or monetary loss due to the information contained within this book; either directly or indirectly.

Legal Notice:
This book is copyright protected. This book is only for personal use. You cannot amend, distribute, sell, use, quote or paraphrase any part, or the content within this book, without the consent of the author or publisher.

Disclaimer Notice:
Please note the information contained within this document is for educational and entertainment purposes only. All effort has been executed to present accurate, up to date, and reliable, complete information. No warranties of any kind are declared or implied. Readers acknowledge that the author is not engaging in the rendering of legal, financial, medical or professional advice.

Table Of Contents

Guided Meditation for Overcoming Anxiety 5

Guided Meditation for Overcoming Anxiety 2 9

Guided Meditation for Sleep 14

Guided Meditation for Deep Sleep 2 17

Guided Meditation for Self-healing 20

Guided Meditation for Self-healing 2 23

Guided Meditation for Relaxation 27

Guided Meditation for Relaxation 2 31

Guided Meditation for Overcoming Insomnia 35

Guided Meditation for Overcoming Depression 38

Guided Meditation for Overcoming Depression 2 43

Guided Mindfulness Meditation for Overcoming Anxiety 46

Guided Meditation For Overcoming Depression 53

Guided Meditation For Stress Relief 61

Guided Meditation for Sleep- The Magic Garden (30 Minutes) 69

Guided Meditation Returning To Sleep (30 Minutes) 72

Guided Meditation for sleep- The Birds Of The Mountain Forest (30 Minutes) 75

Guided Meditation For Sleep & Anxiety Relief (40 Minutes) 78

Guided Meditation for Overcoming Anxiety

Welcome to this guided meditation for overcoming anxiety. This will provide you the ability to free yourself from worries and stress. Practise this session whenever you like, but preferably a time you know you won't be distrubed for 30 minutes or so. Simply find a quiet and comfortable spot. Get yourself into a comfortable position. I would recommend lying on your back, with your hands relaxed by your sides, with your legs relaxed, straight and slightly opened to the ceiling.

Now you are comfortable position, shift you to focus to my voice and simply follow my guidance. As you follow along, this meditation will guide you, helping you release any anxiety, feel relief, and find your place of peace within.

Prepare your body and mind for this meditation, for relaxation. Allow yourself to embrace and enjoy the peace this session provides you, simply from the release of all your anxiety and disturbing thoughts. Allow your thoughts to swiftly pass through. There is no longer a need for them. There is nothing to worry over. Now, you are safe.

Take a nice, deep breath, using your stomach, so your inhale can be as deep as possible. As the air circulates through your body, bring your attention to this moment, to right now. Anxiety is usually the result of placing too much of your focus on the future, on things that haven't happened yet and may never will. As we move foward with this meditation, you will learn how to bring yourself back to this present moment. Right now, this moment is all that existsts. At this moment, all is good.

Right now, there is no better place for you do be. This time, right here, is the right thing for you and your growth. Nothing else is more of a priority than what you are doing now. There is no where else you need to be.

Reassure and trust that all will be fine. Any tension you feel will pass. You will be okay, you will reach a deep state of relaxation, and all will pass.

You deserve all the good in life, to feel great and to let go off all anxiety. Simply remain present in this moment, focusing your undivided attention. Your thoughts don't need to be protected.

Now, bring awareness to your body. Scan through your body placing your focus on each and every part and notice how they feel exactly.

Anxiety is certainly unpleasant. A mechanism to protect yourself, when really it does you more harm. You are in no danger. You are safe. There is no longer room within you to store it anymore.

Now, we will work thorugh the whole body relaxing it, part by part. Slowly work through, scanning your body, focusing on each part, and relaxing it. Notice any signs of tension, where you are holding anxiety in the body. As you come across these areas, try to relax these tense muscles. Breathe deeply allowing your breath to relax you more with every exhale.

Relax your toes and feet. Relax your ankles and legs, up to your knees, relaxing them too. Let your heavy, tight muscles, loosen and relax. Working up to your hips and glutes, relax them. Your lower half of your body is completely relaxed now. Scan it once more, noticing any areas that still cling on to any anxiety. For now, simply observe these areas and we will come back to them in a bit.

Now focus on your stomach. Bring your attention to how relaxed it feels, as it rises and falls with every breath. Then relax your chest. Allow your ribcage to move freely, simply by the air alone.

Now notice your back. How it feels against gravity or whatever surface you lay on. Imagine your spine resting neutrally in perfect alignment. As you breath now, work from the lowest point of your back upwards, gladually relaxing each section. Allow the air as you exhale to remove any tensions and anxiety. Notice any points where anxiety still clings on, and remember exactly where.

Moving up towards your hands, relax them. As your fingertips and palms face up towards the sky, allow them to release anything your holding onto, relaxing them completely. Move up your arms, relaxing your forearms, elbows and upper arms.

Now focus your attention onto your shoulders, relaxing them. Here, is an important aspect of relaxation, as often our shoulders hold most of our worries, stress and axiety. The weight of this negative energy we are not always aware of, and so remains. So, let your shoulders drop, so they rest neutrally allowing your arms to hang weightlessly from them. Release all of the weight you found yourself carrying on your shoulders. Pemit all of those concerns to leave you.

Next relax your neck, feel as the muscles loosen and your head is effortlessly held and supported. Whilst you do this, feel as your throat relaxes becoming seemingly more open. As you continue to move through your body, continue to note any spots that are still tense, making a mental note for later.

It's time to relax your head and face. So, relax the lower face area, such as your jaw and lips, making sure your tongue rests neutrally in its natural position. Let your cheeks and nose relax, allowing every last facial muscle to release and lengthen. Make sure your eyelids rest softly over your eyes and aren't being squeezed shut. Notice how good it feels to let your eyes rest. Relax your eyebrows and forehead, simply letting them rest wherevers natural. Now, relax the top of the head. Take a deep breath, feeling the whole body slip deeper into relaxation.

Now let us scan the body once more, noticing any areas that don't feel completely relaxed yet, anywhere that seems to be holding anxiety. This could be anywhere, your jaw, shoulders, back or even the forehead. Check through all parts of you, locating any anxiety that still remains.

Now, imagine these areas of tension feel hot. Visualize yourself as chocolate, something that has the ability to change state. Feel as those points grow hotter and hotter, and when warm enough, the choclate starts to melt. As your body soothingly melts, feel as your muscles become softer and more elastic, whilst any tension melts away, until they become completely relaxed and anxiety-free.

Enjoy the calming sensations you feel right now. The complete state of peace and lightness you feel, as if you are floating. This relaxation is a gift to yourself. The most beneficial, invaluable gift, you could receive right now.

Scan the whole body once more, this time observing for where in your body feels the most relaxed. Place your focus right here, enjoying the warmth and relaxation of that part. Now, allow this sensation to spread from this area, slowly enveloping the whole body. As this relaxed zone grows, gradually saturating the body, it pushes out all anxiety.

The power of your breath will help you overcome anxiety. This is your most powerful tool, allowing you to overcome many obstacles, calming and relaxing you. So, simply focusing on your breathing is all you need to do. If your thoughts infiltrate your mind, it's okay. Don't fight them, or pass any judgement, simply put them aside. You don't need these thoughts right now.

Now, bring your focus to your breathing. Feel as the cool, refreshing air enters into your nostrils, completely filling and expanding the lungs, before leaving once more as you exhale. Simply focus on your breath alone. Place your hands on your stomach and feel how it rises and falls as the air pours in and out. Feel your lungs emptiness as the air leaves with your exhale.

Stay with your breath. If you begin to feel any anxiety arise, just take another deep breath and allow the steady rhythm of your breathing to calm you, guiding you back to this meditation.

Inhale, counting to four. One, two, three, four.

Then holding your breath, and counting to three.

One, two, three.

Exhale, counting to eight.

One, two, three, four, five, six, seven, eight.

Once more:

Inhale, counting to four.

One, two, three, four.

Hold your breath, counting to three.

One, two, three.

Exhale, counting to eight.

One, two, three, four, five, six, seven, eight.

If your mind brings thoughts distracting you, just observe it for a few moments, then let it go. Use your breath to anchor you to right now, so your focus remains with me.

Imagine the very air you inhale, contains a wonderful peaceful and calming energy, whilst the air you exhale is your anxiety. Each time you breathe out, you are letting go of tension and anxiety, leaving more room for peace and relaxation. Feel as the space for relaxation becomes bigger and bigger, whilst the space filled with anxiety shrinks, gradually becoming smaller and smaller until it exists no more. Just become aware of how your breathing soothes and calms you.

Now, as you inhale, mentally say to yourself: "Relax." Then, as you exhale, repeat "Relax."

Once again, repeat this: inhale - relax, exhale - relax.

Your body is relaxed, and your mind is calm. Your thoughts are slowing now. You are in control. You are completely safe and calm.

Now, let us use this safe environment, this moment just for you, and think about how you feel when you are overwhelmed with anxiety. Understand that it is normal to feel this way when you are concerned. Whenever you next feel this way, remind yourself that it is okay and will pass.

Now, allow your mind to completely relax, too. Riht now, you don't need to focus on anything. Just enjoy this time, with the relaxation it brings you, and trust everything will be fine.

You find yourself in a special place now. A place of inner peace and tranquillity. Here there is no place for worries, no need for them. All is good. You feel relief for these calming sensations, but also, for you have learned how to get here. Just your breath and focus have brought you here. This place remains within you, and you can access it whenever you wish. Here, you will always find shelter and rest, away from your worries and anxiety.

Feel free to carry these feelings with you, even after you finish this meditation. Allow this peace to stay with you throughout your day, as you complete all you need to.

When you next feel anxiety start to take over your mind, try to remeber this meditation as this may be enough to ground you in peace. This in mind, you will be able to remain in control and release any anxiety. Simply by breathing deeply, allowing the air you take in to relax you and bring yourself to the true present moment. With your practice of this meditation, your confidence will only grow. You will know you are bigger than anything that causes your anxiety, that you can remain in control.

You are powerful. You are calm. You are free. You are peaceful. You are strong. You are hopeful. You are full of positivity. You are rejuvenated.

Now, for those of you who want to return to your day, filled with its usual tasks, when this meditation is over, it's time to wake up. So, slowly wiggle your fingers and toes and gently stretch. Whenever you feel ready, slowly open your eyes. You will take this peace with you throughout your day.

But for those of you who want to move into sleep now: continue to enjoy these feelings of relaxation allowing them to guide you into a restful sleep. Once you wake, you will feel refreshed and renewed, calm, and at peace. Sleep well, and enjoy your dreams.

Guided Meditation for Overcoming Anxiety 2

Welcome to this guided meditation for the relief of anxiety, replacing it with inner peace and balance. As you move through this meditation, you will learn how to detach yourself from any disturbing emotions enabling you to find serenity.

Now as we begin, simply prepare your body for this session. Get yourself into a comfortable position. Feel free to lie on your back or side or to sit, whatever you find most comfortable. You don't have to remain here in this position for the whole meditation, you can easily change if you find yourself in any discomfort. Only you know what is best for you.

This time is only for you. A gift to yourself. You deserve this time, simply for yourself.

Often those who suffer from anxiety, spend too much time in their head, focusing on thoughts so they are mentally absent. You may find your mind is hyperactive, chaotically busy, focused internally on your future. This means your mind doesn't give much attention to the sensations of your physical body and neglects your breathing. Perhaps your breathing rhythm is constantly short and shallow, as if you are facing real dangers constantly.

Through your practice of meditation, you will learn how to relax your body, slow your mind, and deepen your breathing, allowing you to change your current patterns in life. As you develop this skill of relaxation, your brain will understand you are safe, so it can switch off the panic button, releasing you from your anxiety.

We will also use some mantras to change your unproductive beliefs, allowing you to remove any subconscious blockages.

So follow my invitation to join me now. Simply close your eyes and follow my voice. Bring your attention to this very moment.

Now, focus on your head. Become aware of your muscles that make up your forehead and scalp, and take a moment to contract them. Then, allow them to relax. Moving down, feel any tension you hold in your eyelids, squeeze and and then relax them. Release and let go, calming and relaxing you. Relax all the muscles in the face. Then moving to your lips, tightly compress them, before letting them relax so they lay softly closed. Clench your jaw, then relax. Press your chin against your chest to tense the muscles in the back of your neck. Then slowly bring your head back up, relaxing it.

Contract your shoulder muscles, and then relax them, let them loosen allowing the shoulders to hang freely in a relaxed position.

Moving to your fists, hands and arms clench them tightly. Then release this force you hold over them, relaxing them all.

Tense the muscles in your back and then release, relaxing them, notice as they loosen, one by one, until your whole back feels lighter and relaxed. Take a deep breath in, filling your chest with air, and while you exhale, feel the muscles in your ribcage relaxing.

Pull your head and spine upwards towards the sky, feeling your abdominals tense. Then let your stomach become relaxed.

Contract your glutes, so they become firm before slowly relaxing them. Notice how you body is becoming filled with relaxation.

Finally pay attention to your leg as a whole, contracting it from the very top by your hips, to the thighs and down to the feet and toes. Then release, relaxing every part: your hips, your thighs, your knees, ankles and feet. Simply allow relaxation to take over all.

Now enjoy the sensation of complete relaxation throughout your whole body.

Moving foward, shift your focus to your breath. For now don't change a thing. Just become aware of your current cycle of breath, in and out.

Now your body is relaxed and free from any anxiety, let us use the power of your imagination to work on freeing your mind from any anxiety as well. So, visualize yourself lying on a bed of soft grass. It is a beautiful day with a clear blue sky, and the sun above soothingly warms you. Take a deep breath now and as you exhale, imagine you breathe out soap bubbles. These bubbles are filled with all your anxiety from your whole body. As you breathe out these bubbles, watch as they float away, into the sky before they pop, releasing your anxiety into the sky above.

Inhale once more, and as you do so collect all the anxiety you can find. Imagine blowing it into a bubble, just like a piece of gum and imagine blowing it into a huge bubble. Now eject this bubble, into the sky. The bubble bounces in the air upwards, far away until it finally pops out.

Repeat this process once again. Inhale deeply, expanding your stomach as you do so. Then breathe out a healthy jet of bubbles, filled with all of your anxiety. They fly all around you, glistening with the suns reflection, and taking your anxiety far from your reach. You watch as they pop and exist no more.

Now as you inhale, round up all the anxiety that still clings to you. Exhale, releasing another stream of bubbles. Watch as your worries and anxiety are now in complete control of nature, the wind slowly popping them one by one.

Now focus on the affirmations I say. Slowly repeat them to yourself, mentally or out loud, whichever you wish. Dedicate a breath to each and every one.

Inhale deeply, and repeat the mantra as you exhale.

I am aware of my breathing. I am aware of the air flowing in and out of my body.

Inhale. Exhale.

I am aware of my worries, fears and anxiety. I am aware of how they make me feel.

I'm aware of these negative thoughts and how they influence my anxiety.

I'm aware of my body's rhythem. I'm aware of the steady pace of my heart.

Between each beat, make space for the focus on your breathing alone.

Now, while I inhale and exhale, my mind slowly becomes quieter and more calm.

I am releasing all negative thoughts.

As I breath, my anxiety is calmed.

I am sinking deeper into relaxation, both my body and mind.

With every exhale, I release all my fears and worries.

With every inhale, I find yet more peace and calmness.

I inhale tranquility. I exhale anxiety.

As I'm aware of my breathing, I let go of all that doesn't serve me.

Smile as you breathe, I deserve all the best from life.

I inhale serenity. I exhale pain.

I am completely safe and grounded. I allow myself to cherish in this peace.

I am strong.

With each day, things will only get better.

I expect and am prepared for great things to come my way.

Now allow your anxiety to feel valid, tell your anxiety: I see you. I hear you. I accept you, and love you for all you are.

I allow myself to experiance all my emotions without pushing any aside. Emotions don't define me, they are just a small part of me. I can observe all emotions while reminaing calm.

Rather than rejecting and fighting against emotions, I accept them. As I do so, the load I carry around with me reduces and I feel lighter and more free. As you set them free, emotions simply flow through your body before they leave you.

Repeat to yourself , "Thank you for your help in protecting me. But I no longer need your help, as I am ready to move foward alone, liberated and free to do as I wish."

Enjoy how much more lighter and free you feel now.

I work on healing all the time, my body and mind in perfect harmony.

I grant myself this wonderful sensation of complete peace.

Now using your mind's eyes, envision you are bathing in a soothing, warm, golden light. This powerful yet gentle light healing your every part, all the way from your head to your toes. This light hugging you gently in its soft glow.

I enjoy this sensation, as if I am being wrapped in a soft, warm blanket. I feel completely safe and at peace. It's so good to feel the warm, soft glow kiss my skin.

I feel refreshed and re-energized now.

I feel wellness as it has seeped into my whole body, into each and every cell of my being.

I unwind in the comfort and peace of right here. I allow myself to absorb all this energy, revitalizing and replenishing myself with this peace.

I enjoy this moment and this completely relaxed state, free from any worries and stress.

Now, imagine you are stood at the top of a set of stairs. Picture them however you wish, winding down spirally, made of glass so you can see right below, it doesn't matter. You are simply going to move down them.

Take a deep in. As you do so count to three. One, two, three.

Now exhale, you are ready to go downstairs now, as you do so count your steps to five. One, two, three, four, five.

Pause as you inhale, counting to four. One, two, three, four.

Exhale, moving on down the stairs, counting to six now. One, two, three, four, five, six.

Pause, inhale, counting to five. One, two, three, four, five.

Exhale, moving down, counting to seven. One, two, three, four, five, six, seven.

You find yourself in a dark room now. It may be dark but you can see just enough that you know where you're going. Don't be afraid of this unknown darkness. You are safe. You are in control.

You take a few steps foward and find yourself in the centre of a room. Calmly you take a seat with your legs crossed on the cool floor. Although you can barely see, you sense an item on the floor, just infront of you. Leaning foward you pick up a small, wooden bowl.

Now, as you hold it in your hands. It's more heavy and steady than you imagined and as you run your fingers over its smooth surface you notice it is completely empty. As if waiting patiently for someone to fill it with something.

You place it gently back on the floor infront of you.

You take a moment to visualize your anxiety, a dark sand weighing down your body.

Now, you sift through your body, rounding up any sand that is lurking within you, before placing it into the bowl infront. You repeat this a few times grabbing any grains that remian inside you.

Picture your worries and stresses as icy, black stones that sit in your mind. Simarily to your anxiety, take them and place them into the bowl too. This bowl may seem small, but trust that all that has been holding you back can fit inside.

Repeat this, placing every last worry that has been bothering you, and causing your anxiety into the bowl infront. Finally, all you anxiety, stresses and negative thoughts are in the bowl.

Breathe in deeply, using your belly.

Everything is in constant movement, things constantly changing.

The dark can turn into light.

Your concerns and anxiety can change into love, peace, strength, and happiness.

Notice the bowl now. It has become much lighter and seems to glow more with your every breath. The dark sand and stones grow lighter too. The stones shining brightly like rare jewels and the sand glistening, illuminating this dark space. The bowl radiates a bright, golden light that fills the room. Now you find yourself sat in bright, clean light, absorbing it in.

Not only have your surroundings undergone change, your thoughts have too. They are no longer dark and heavy, but are shimmering, priceless jewels of luck, hope and wonderful possibilities. As you inhale, your whole body absorbs this bright, healing, empowering light. Now you glow softly, attracting more healing energy to you. You are in complete peace.

As you enjoy the wonders this room brings you, a dark thought may sneak up on you. Here you can simply direct it into the bowl infront. The bowl is here for you. The bowl can hold all the negativity you carry on your shoulders.

This room is always here, ready for you if you need to unload. So feel free to return if ever you wish.

Now, whenever you are ready, stand up, and slowly make you way back up the stairs. This time as you go upwards, take this light and jewles of positive thought with you as you go.

Now as we go upstairs, take a deep breath and count backwards with me.

Six, five, four, three, two, one.

You have arrived back where you started, although now you feel changed. You feel liberated from you worries and anxiety, which has now been replaced with peace and tranquility. Now you spread light with you as you move, and understand that whenever you need more you can return here.

Now when your ready, take a deep breath in. Exhale and slowly open your eyes. Thank you for joining me today.

Guided Meditation for Sleep

Good evening. Welcome to the meditation that will guide you into a peaceful nights sleep. All you need to do is get comfortable and focus on my voice which will lead you into a state of deep relaxation, and this can decieve even the most busy minds into a restful sleep.

You may find yourself drifting off as I speak. If this happens, don't worry. Although you may be asleep, your subconscious mind is still listening and being influenced by the positivity this meditation brings. So, you will still become relaxed on a deeper level, improving the quality of your sleep.

This day is no longer here. All you have experianced today is over, slowly drifting into your past. So now, simply give yourself to this moment. Remain present here, as there is nothing else you should be doing now. In this moment, all you shoulde be doing is enjoying the comfortable warmth of your bed. The night is here so you can rest and recover from your day, readying you for tomorrow. Your body and mind have been busy in use all day, so now is the time to give them a break and re-energize. This guided meditation will take you into a state ensuring you can rejuvenate and refresh. So now, listen to me and allow yourself to relax. Let your body take charge, relaxing at whatever pace it desires. With each breath, you can relax your body, part by part or simply as a whole.

So, simply remain present, to right here and now. Enjoy the warmth and peace this moment brings you. Feel as your pillow softly hugs your head, and the warm blanket enwraps you. Feel as your body melts into the comfort of your mattress

Now, shift your focus to your breath. Using your stomach, take a deep breath. Feel as the cool, refreshing air flows through your nostrils straight into your lungs. Then notice how this air travels back out of your body, out through your mouth. With each breath, inhale deeper and deeper. With each exhale, feel as you sinker deeper in your bed.

Smile, you are taking this time to care for yourself, to relax and recharge. Breathe in, breathe out, diving deeper into relaxation as you go. Embrace the soft touch of your bedding, how it gets more and more comfortable with each breath. As you lie here, enjoy the pleasant sensations this moment brings you. Breathe in, breath out and greet the feeling of deep relaxation.

Now feel free to imagine you are in a warm, cozy nest completely safe, or that your are peacefully floating in a boat on calm ocean waters. Whichever one you gravitate towards, you are cradled tenderly, simply listening to the water or the sounds of a gentle breeze, with your eyes resting closed.

You feel at ease, simply enjoying this moment. Breathing in, and out, you smile to yourself as you appreciate the beauty of right here. and the joy. Breathe in, breathe out, and smile to this moment and to yourself. This moment is beautiful.

Take a nice deep breath. It is time to relax the entire body now. So move your focus throughout your body, paying attention to each and every part, relaxing each. To begin, start with your toes and feet. Relax them completely before moving on up to your lower legs and knees. Feel your legs open up to the ceiling, as they accept this relaxation. Next, move up to the thighs, hips and glutes, relaxing each. Now relax your hands, starting from the fingertips, to the palms and finally the wrists. Relax your arms now too.

Bring your focus to your stomach, how it gently rises and falls with your inhale and exhale. Take another deep breath, turning your attention to your chest as you exhale. How your chest completey empties and your chest muscles become relaxed.

Now, become aware of your whole back. How are you currently holding it? Imagine now each vetebrae in perfect alignment. Observe each, starting from the base of your spine, simply relaxing each one as you move upwards, feeling just like a soothing massage. Take a deep breath in, feeling the air flow right through your spine as you exhale.

Relax your shoulders. Release all you've been carrying around with you, throughout your day. Do you have any worries? Leg them go. Are you holding any tension? If so, let it go. Are you holding onto any anger or resentment? Let that go too. As you release all negativity you have been carrying with you, feel as your shoulders become lighter and more free, now they are released of all that extra weight.

Open up your airway, relaxing the inside of your throat. Notice the back of your neck, allow it to relax supported by your soft pillow. Give your neck some relief from holding your head up all day. It deserves this time now, simply for rest.

Pay attention to your head now, granting it this relaxation. Yours ears work constantly, even through the night, so give them all the relaxation they need. Notice how you are holding your jaw. Let your jaw release. All you need to focus on is your body moving deeper into relaxation. So, relax the tongue, lips and cheeks, allowing them to rest without tension. Move to your forehead and eyebrows, making sure they are holding no tension and simply becoming more relaxed. Lastly let your eyelids lay calmly over your tired eyes. They deserve a good rest right now as well, so enjoy the sensation as they sink further into your head.

Finally, let us focus on the body as a whole. Give the very surface of the body the opportunity to relax. Visualize your skin and relax it too, for it needs to recharge and rejuvenate as well. Now imagine the inside of your body. Observe all your organs that work for you all the time. Mentally send them your love and care, allowing them to relax.

Moving foward its time to work on relaxing your mind now. Give yourself permission to let go of any emotions that crowd your mind. Release all sadness, anger, jealousy, any fears or worries- just let them go. These emotions are valid, so don't be hard on yourself. You deserve your own forgiveness for any of your mistakes, so just let go. Overthinking or holding that grudge is only slowing your progress, so forgive yourself and let go. Accept any of these emotions, they are simply part of the learning process.

Your mind is likely busy with thoughts, running through chaotically. Try your best to let them pass through you. It is expected that thoughts and pictures may cross your mind as your trying to relax. Just observe them, setting them aside for another time. Now, these thoughts are not needed. Right here, you have nothing to do. There is no task, or anything for you to accomplish. The night is here, simply for your productive rest. The best thing you can do right now is allow your body this time for a rewarding recharge.

Now, imagine your mind operating just like a spinning wheel. Spinning round quickly at the pace of your thoughts. Visualize this wheel and its speed, how it gradually slows. It continues to gently slow, until finally it reaches a stop. Your mind now calm, clear as it has slipped into a deep state of relaxation. Now, ready to move into it's dreamy state.

Take a deep breath, as you exhale, let go of all you don't need, all you don't love and all that holds you back. As this negativity is released and your mind more clear, allow the inner light and clarity to spread throughout your body.

If your mind brings up any thoughts or emotions, continue to let them pass through, without your engagement. Stay calm. Stay present. Simply remain in this moment, as you slip further into relaxation.

Focus on your breathing without the urge to change anything. Observe its deep steady rhythm as you enjoy feeling cozy, at peace, in a warm nest or floating calmly in a boat.Do nothing but simply enjoying this moment.

Inhale deeply. Then exhale, feeling again how your body relaxes on a deeper level. All you carry that you dont need, fades away. You are carefree. Now all you feel is calm, peace and easiness.

Inhale, Exhale.

Right now, you have all the time in the world for just you. There is no where to rush to. Everything you could possibly need is right with you. You are in the right place, where everything happens as you need. Time is of no limit now. All is good.

Hand over all your worries and stresses. Leave everything to a higher power, and trust that all will be well and fall into place perfectly.

Allow your inner smile to be released, smiling to yourself and life.

Feel as you are liberated from your worries. Embracing the serenity and carefreeness of here, finding nothing but harmony in this moment.

Breathe in, breathe out. Feel a soothing comfort, just like your body and your mind are visiting a mental spa.

Drift deeper now, into sleep. Trust that all is well, and allowing yourself into this dreamy state.

Sleep well, and enjoy your sweet dreams.

Guided Meditation for Deep Sleep 2

Good evening. Welcome to this meditation, which will prepare you for a restful nights sleep. So, let's get started straight away by making yourself comfortable in wherever you plan to sleep. Make yourself as warm and comfortable as you can. All you need to do is let my voice guide you, although don't stress if you find yourself asleep before I finish. Sometimes sleep comes fast and easily, whereas other times it seems to never come. It's okay if you don't slip into sleep during the meditation. Either way, your body and mind will enjoy this time to rest and relax, exactly the same as if you were asleep.

Simply allow yourself to remian present in this exact moment. This time, is simply for rest, so you can recover from your day. Relish the comfort your bed provides you with. You you sink into your pillows and mattress, fully supported. Feel the peace and warmth of right here. You are thankful your day has passed and appreciate all the good this day brought you. But for now, it is time to let go, allow this day to enter your past, so you can stay entirely in the present.

Shift your focus to your breath. Inhale slowly and deeply, noticing how the air flows through your body and back out again as you exhale. Sense any tense parts of your body. For now, this is the time for your complete relaxation. As you exhale, feel the top of your head start to relax. Breathe in, and breathe out, relaxing your cheeks and jaw now. With your next breath, turn you attention to your mouth, noticing as this cool, refreshing air relaxes your throat. Inhale. Exhale, relaxing your lips, tongue and cheeks. Notice any tension you are holding in your forehead and eyebrows. Breathe in, before breathing them all out, letting them relax. With your next breath relax your eyelids, allowing them to rest calmly over your eyes. Exhale, relaxing your whole head once again.

Take a deep breath, becoming aware of how you are holding your neck. Exhale, relaxing all the muscles there. Relax the front, sides and back allowing your pillow to fully support your head. Your neck has done all it needs today. Now, all it needs is rest.

Inhale using your stomach, and exhale feeling your shoulders drop and relax. Release all the weight you've been carrying through the day, let it be swept up by your breath.

Breathe in, allowing your lungs to be filled with air. Breathe out, letting your chest deflate and drop down, completely relaxed.

Inhale again, filling the stomach with air. Exhale, letting your stomach sink, relaxing completely.

Now as you breathe in, notice how the muscles of your back feel. Exhale, relaxing all the muscles in your lower back. Take another breath in and exhale, this time relaxing all the muscles in your upper back. Breath in, devoting this breath to your back as a whole. Visualize how all the tesnion from your back is released through your spine.

Now moving on, pay attention to all the tension you're holding in your around your hip level. Exhale, releasing all. Relax your hips. Relax all that's here on your body.

Breathe in, and feel as the air begins to target the tension in your legs.

Exhale, allowing your glutes, thighs and calves to relax.

Inhale. Exhale, and feel your entire legs relax. As they do so, let them drift open and face up to the ceiling. Allow your ankles and feet this relaxation. Relax your toes. Take a deep breath, and exhale noticing your entire legs are now completely relaxed.

Inhale deeply, notice any tension that remains within you, let it all go with your exhale.

Now, imagine you find yourself on a mountain in a beautiful, enchanting forest. The late afternoon sun beams through the leaves overhead, glistening in spots every few steps. You have had a tiring day, walking through nature. Notice how the green leaves of the trees sway gently in the breeze, as you make your way down the small, winding narrow path. The birds make a peaceful, calming song whilst the whole forest listens, appreciating its beauty. You are tired.

Your legs lazily continue on this pathway. They need rest.

You move downhill, carried by its push rather than your own legs. Whilst you are here your mind keeps drifting to the thought of a cozy pillow and soft blanket. You feel sleepiness take over, and you begin to yawn.

This day is nearly over, the sun looking to retire from yet another day. The evening is closing in. The birds sing their gentle song, preparing to settle in their warm nests for the night. You would love to lay down right here, soothed by the forest. But you have to keep moving foward, down and round, so you can make it to the cottage before the sun goes down, placing the forest into darkness. The path leads you straight to the cottage, straight to sleep. As you move the forest is peaceful. The gentle sounds of this place- the soft rustle of the leaves and grass, the relaxing birds song and even the sound of your steps as you move foward, makes you more and more sleepy.

You move steadily down the path, wishing you will reach the cottage soon. Your legs are tired and all you seek is to sink into your warm, comfortable bed and rest.

Now take a deep breath in, and start to count each step you make down this path and through the forest. Inhale, counting to four. Exhale, counting your steps down the path: one, two, three, four, five, six.

You are yawing now, ready for the comfort of your bed. Inhale again, counting to four: one, two, three, four. Exhale, counting your steps down the path: one, two, three, four, five, six. Evening has arrived. The forest becomes slowly darker and darker. The sounds of the forest begin to settle, becoming quiet. As if it is now time for nature to sleep. There is no longer beams of sunlight shining through the trees, but instead the soft glow of the moon and stars in the dark sky. You are so close to the cottage now, just a few more steps. Your legs feel heavy and your body is about to fall asleep. Your mind is calm and clear, soothed by the enchanting forest.

You are here now. You open the door of the warm cottage. Take a nice, slow, deep breath. As you exhale, count. One, two, three, four, five, six. You are so sleeping now counting is difficult. Inhale. Exhale. One, two, three, four, five, six. You are finally at your bed now. You lay down, your body sinking into the cozy mattress and pillows. Your bed soothes your tired body. It is time to sleep now.

Your feet are sleeping. Your heavy leg muscles gently falling asleep too. You relax allowing yourself to fall into sleep. Your back muscles soften and are sleeping. Your head is relaxed and sleeping. Your eyes, gently covered by your eyelids are sleeping. Your body is falling asleep, part by part. Finally, your whole body is sleeping now. Your mind asleep and emotion free. Goodnight.

Guided Meditation for Self-healing

Welcome to the meditation for self-healing. Whether you don't feel well, have or are looking for a diagnosis, or suffer from chronic pain, this meditation is for you. This will help you use your body's ability to heal itself. During this meditation, I will guide you into a deeply relaxed state. From this state, you will then have the opportunity to truely talk to your body, sending it love and empowering it to heal.

To maximize your self-healing, practice this meditation as often as possible. You can heal no matter the time of day. So even if you fall asleep during, your sunconscious is still following along with the meditation, aiding your body in its self-healing.

So to begin, get yourself into a comfortable position. You should be pleasantly warm, so no discomfort can disrupt the session. Allow yourself this time to simply relax. Place your hand over your heart, feel its beat and allow it to guide you into relaxation. As your body begins to relax, notice how it begins to soften.

Now, imagine a warm, golden light spread through your body. It infiltrates through your muscle tissues sinking right into your bones. This golden light, travels up through your feet, to your lower legs, knees, moving gradually up your thighs and hips. It doesn't stop here; it moves through to your stomach before slowly encompassing your entire body. Feel as this warm, soothing light spreads through your hands, arms, shoulders, neck and back. Enjoy the relaxing sensation it brings. Right now, the best thing you could be doing is bathing in this golden, healing light. Knowing just this, continue to allow relaxation to seep in, until your whole body is completely relaxed and you feel as if you are floating. Your whole body is filled with the bright, golden light. This light has coated every organ, every system, radiating in all directions, and shining out through your skin.

The negativity, all toxins and unproductive emotions you carry hide in the darkness within you. This light you are now illuminated with transforms any areas of darkness, placing it into light and therefore relieving you of the weight you carry on your shoulders. Now all your negative thoughts, doubts and concerns no longer have a place to reside inside of you. There is no longer a place for anger, jealousy and hatred to hide, no corner to linger anymore.

Now, imagine you are taking a walk through nature, on a warm summers evening. The air is a perfect, cool temperature. Around you you hear the chirp of the crickets in the grass, and the soothing sound of the bird's song overhead. You walk down a small, narrow path, trees and flowers growing alongside, gently swaying in the breeze. The path flows away, carrying you with it.

As you've been carried down this path, you now find yourself stood before a large tree. This tree may be old, but strong and healthy, it offers large branches as a home for many. Birds, squirrels and insects enjoy calling this tree home, whilst most animals enjoy some relief from the sun on hot, summers days by sitting underneath it. This tree towers over all others near, whilst its roots spread deep into the ground, connecting to the source of life. Take a step forward and place your hand on the tree trunk infront of you. Imagine you are absorbing some of this trees mighty life power. Feel yourself connect with this higher intelligence, this tree has been able to absorb from touching the sky. Notice as you become more and more grounded, just like the deep roots of this tree. Feel as the powerful, green energy flows through you, right from the top of your head, down to the tips of the toes.

Now you find yourself sat down under the tree. Leaning up against the tree, you listen to the sounds of nature. The green wood behind you fully supports you, allowing you to shift your focus to your body. Take a deep breath and simply appreciate your body for all it does for you every single day. Think about every last way it supports you, even when you are at rest. You are thankful for this higher intelligence that works within your body, beating your heart and pumping blood through your veins. Digesting your food and nourishing your every cell and managing all systems within you. It protects you from the outer world and holding your wonderful soul. Take this moment to appreciate all that, consciously telling your body "I Love you". The world works by responding to the vibration of love, plants, animals even water responds to love. Your body is not an exception. So feel as your body responds to these words, to this love and affection.

Now, thank your legs for carrying you, on your journey through this beautiful world. Thank your hands for serving you for so long already. Thank your back for holding you straight and supporting you. Thank your neck for holding your head, assisting in every precious movement of your head. Thank you stomach and digestive system, for digesting all the food you eat. You feel truly blessed, you are able to move, run, jump and trust that your body does all it needs for you. Thank your brain, for being with you at all times, assisting you in all ways and simply being a powerful central. Thank your mouth enabling you to express yourself, feel tastes, laugh and kiss. Thank your nose for helping you breathe and notice wonderful scents. Thank you eyes for providing you with vision, so you can see amazing things. Just let all this gratefulness sink in.

Now, repeat these words I say, mentally or out loud: Body, I love you. I accept and appreciate all of you. I know you perform as best you can. I wish you great health. You deserve the best, so you can function perfectly. I enwrap you in my love, for you are amazing. My love seeps into every organ, every tissue, and every bone. My love circulates through every system and every cell because I truly love all they do for me. I give you my blessing, so energy and good health can flow through me.

I trust you. I trust in your ability to heal yourself. So, I invite your wisdom and power to do as you know best, for you.

Take a few deep, purposeful breaths. Then allow the air from your breath to flow through you as it normally would. Allow the healing power of your breath to settle throughout your body. Feel as this infinite love and gratitude spreads through you now. You have all you need to heal.

Allow these wonderful sensations to remain within you. Feel as these sensations of love, purity and calmness spreads, softening and warming you, starting right from your heart. Feel unconditional and eternal love. Feel completely grounded and complete. Enjoy this sensation. Let this feeling spread from your heart, slowly growing throughout your entire being. Simply let your body soak it all up.

Now, observe how your body feels, noticing any area of your body that may need some extra love and care. Pour love into that part in particular, which may need some more help in healing. Imagine a warm, golden, healing light pours into that part, overwhelming it with its shining power. This part of you is bathed in light, removing all its issues and pain that usually settles in the darkness here. This light brings perfect balance and harmony, giving this part the special attention it requires. This light heals and soothes not only this part but your whole body. It restores a perfect equilibrium, so your body has the perfect conditions is needs, as if you've been reborn! Your body deserves to work at its best, and absolure health is the best natural condition to allow this. You are created to be unique, complex and absolutely healthy. Only your body knows just how to restore all functions and cure itself.

Enjoy the peacefulness of this moment. Feel how your body responds to this wonderful, relaxed state. Your body is thankful for this opportunity you have given to it. It is grateful for this time and care but also the trust you have placed in it. Right here, is the best place for your body to be. A safe space full of peace, calmness, serenity, a time with no worries, and therefore a respite from stress. This space refreshes and rejuvenates your body allowing it to gain the energy it needs to heal itself. You body is so grateful for this time, it will reward you by healing and continuing to be there for you.

Whenever you feel overwhelmed or trapped in pain arising from a health issue, visualize this powerful, healing, golden light enwrapping your body, sending love and energy for that part to heal. Your body knows how to realign itself into harmony, all you need to do is trust in its power and provide it the time and care it needs. Your body and I thank you for this time.

Guided Meditation for Self-healing 2

Welcome to the guided meditation for self-healing. Get yourself into a comfortable position, I recommend lying down, with earphones in so you can fully engage in your healing. The only thing you need to do is to accept healing energy, allowing it to enter every part of your body. After this meditation, let this energy remian within you, continuing to heal you for hours and even days.

So, simply allow yourself 30 minutes, where you can remain completely undisturbed.

Before this healing journey begins, let's prepare by calming yourself with some short breathing exercises. So, inhale through your nose, counting to six. One, two, three, four, five, six. Then exhale, out through your mouth, whilst counting to ten. One, two, three, four, five, six, seven, eight, nine, ten. If you find you can't reach those numbers, that's okay. Just do as your body needs.

Repeat this process again. And then, let your breathing return to its usual slow and steady rhythm. As you inhale, imagine you take in a beautiful, glistening light. Breathing out, exhale all the negativity and worries you carry with you. Notice how relaxed and lighter your body feels with every breath.

Picture yourself now, lying on a bed of soft green grass, in a beautiful garden full of colourful flowers. You lay listening to the sound of this place, the gentle chirp of insects, the soft rustling of grass in the wind and the birds as they sing. You feel peace and serenity wash over you.

Now, moving foward, we will begin to relax the entire body. Slowly take a deep breath in. Shifting your focus to your feet. Relax your toes, arch, heels, and your whole feet. Moving upwards now, relax your ankles, lower legs and knees. Enjoy the sensation as they become relaxed. Bring your focus to your thighs, the sides, front and back. Feel as they become more and more relaxed with each exhale. Now, your toes, heels and feet – relaxed. Your ankles, legs, knees and thighs- relaxed.

Place your attention to your hips, glutes, and pelvic area, now. Relax your glutes and observe how, with your every breath, your glutes and hips become looser, more relaxed and yet more free. With them the whole lower body feels the sensations relaxation brings them also.

Now, shift your awareness to your hands. Notice how you are holding them currently, and relax. Allow your fingers to return to their natural curved position, as they do so. Relax your wrists, your forearms, your elbows, and your upper arms. Feel as your arm dangles weightlessly from your shoulders – completely relaxed.

Bring your focus to your main body, to your stomach and chest. Notice how they move easily along to the rythm of your breath. Inhale, and then relax your chest and stomach completely. Move to your lower back, noticing the surface under your back. Slowly relax your back, part by part, starting from the base of your spine, gradually moving up, all the way to the shoulders.

Enjoy the peace this moment provides. Notice how thankful your body is for recieving this calming moment. Feel how much good is happening right now!

Now, moving to the most crucial area to relax in your body, the shoulders. Here you hold the most tension, and carry the weight of most your negative thoughts and energy. So relax them, let them be loose. Observe how they become more relaxed and free with each exhale. Feel as this weight is lifted, your whole body becomes energized and refreshed, liberated from the pain and negativity holding you back.

Now, relax your neck. Relax you jaw, letting it loose. Allow your lips to sit calmly shut, your tongue resting wheres natural- completely relaxed. Relax your cheeks. Relax your eyes, your eyelids laying peacefuly over them. Relax your foreheaf. Relax the very top of your head. Now completely relaxed.

Take a deep breath, allowing the sense of peace to wash over you. Your body now completely relaxed.

Now, envision you are laying under a small, white cloud. This fluffy cloud with its idylic shape is beautiful. This cloud is here, just for you. It floats just above your head, bringing you healing power. Does it fill you with excitement? Do you feel happiness approaching?

The rain starts to drop pure droplets of light, healing rain on you. Feel these soothing drops as they fall on your face. Imagine this healing energy as small crystals, golden light or pure water, however you wish. Simply absorb and connect with its healing properties.

Feel as this healing energy beams down, enwrapping your whole head. Enjoy the sensations this energy brings. You know just what this magical cloud is doing now. It moves down to your neck. You feel as rainfrops now fall on your neck, it now becoming illumintaed with a light. Now, your head and neck are shining.

The cloud gradually makes its way down, to right above your shoulders, chest and stomach. You feel as this gentle rain touches your skin, blessing you with its healing energy. The cloud is expanding to above your arms now. Your arms and hands begin to shine as they are touched by this rain. The cloud grows, it's now above your hips, pelvis and glutes. These parts are bathed in this healing light now. Now, the cloud moves down, raindrops falling on your legs. Notice as they begin to shine themseleves. Observe the rain now, sense its purpose for you, and how it serves you. The white, healing cloud is now above you, covering your whole body, and every part in its healing raindrops. Your head is shining, your neck, shoulders, chest, stomach, arms and legs too. This rain falls on you now, a rain of light, a rain of health, and you shine brightly. Thank all this moment brings to you. You are grateful for all the healing happening right now. If you are currently facing any health issues, bring this white cloud directly on to that part, focusing its energy here. If you don't have any health issues, continue to let the rain fall over your entire body, enjoying its refreshing energy. Simply, visualize yourself shining.

This healing cloud works wonders on you. Now, you are shining brightly from its energy and your every cells brings its thanks for restoring balance in your body. Your body deserves this love and care that you have invited in now.

This time you have granted yourself, is an incredible gift to your body. Your body is thankful, and will show that in its improved performance. Enjoy this moment and your knowledge of the haeling thats occuring within your right now.

You feel comforted in every cell and every atom of your body as this light spreads through you. Any tension that remains in the body is now released, there is no longer a dark place to hide inside you. As the light rain drops fall on you, you skin may tingle or become warm. You feel all your stresses and pain, drain out of you, exactly where these drops of light have landed.

This soft light envelops you, its warm, powerful and soothing.

Enjoy the rain and all the feelings and relaxation it brings to you. Rest in it now, trusting in its work of healing you right now.

Notice as the light radiates from the center of your body. You are filled with pure, loving energy.

Now you are in this relaxed state, your body can heal itself using the infinite wisdom its recieved. As you allow this healing to take place, send yourself loving thoughts to aid this process. Utilize this moment to release the negative thinking patterns you were stuck in, that created the perfect environment for disease to flourish. This will enable you to adopt a new, healthy cycle of thinking, so you can build the perfect environment for perfect, vibrant health.

Now listen as I repeat some positive statements. Allow these ideas to enter your subconscious, allowing the growth of new positive patterns that allow health to flourish in your body and mind.

Feel free to repeat my words mentally or just simply listen to these affirmations, whilst they become your new beliefs.

I am healing my body and mind.

I am worthy of perfect health.

I forgive all I need to forgive.

I forgive myself.

I feel a growing love for myself.

I am full of life.

I take care of myself because I love myself.

I choose health for my body, mind, and spirit.

I am grateful for my amazing body and all it does every day.

I am grateful for my body and mind's health.

I am strong and powerful.

I am completely healthy to the last cell.

I am full of positive energy.

I am calm yet vibrant.

I am loved. I am enough. I am complete.

I am healing and growing.

I am letting go of everything that doesn't serve me.

I am letting go of fear, of anger, jealousy, guilt, pain and tension.

I am in peace. With no need to struggle.

I am an amazing expression of life.

I have power within me, the same power that created me.

Now, I allow that power to heal my body and mind.

The past has no power over me.

I am letting go of all now.

I am unique and wonderful.

I am worthy of love, a birthright.

I accept and appreciate myself.

I'm willing to use the energy to heal. I deserve all the best life can give. I deserve perfect health.

I am in perfect balance and in harmony with the world around me. I allow divine energy to circulate throughout my being, using its higher intelligence to heal.

Take a nice deep breath using your stomach and exhale. Notice how calm and at peace you feel. Now, whenever your ready, gently leave this meditation. Enjoy the rest of your day or, if your wish drift off into a peaceful sleep. Thank you.

Guided Meditation for Relaxation

Welcome to the meditation for reaching deep relaxation. This practice is perfect for whenever you are feeling tense or if you just simply want some time for relaxation and calmness.

Allow my voice to gently guide you to a state of deep relaxation. From there, you can easily drift off to sleep or move on with your day feeling calm and refreshed.

Find a quiet space, you can settle down in for half an hour. Get yourself into a comfortable position, sitting or lying, however you wish. Close your eyes. And allow yourself to journey into relaxation.

Take a deep breath in through your nose, and into your belly. Hold the breath for a moment, then, slowly exhale out through your mouth. Continue to do this, breathing out more slowly than your inhales, allowing your body to feel relaxed as you do so. This air works as a signal to your mind, alerting it that you are completely safe and well. So use this technique whenever you need to slow down and relax.

Breathe in. And slowly breathe out.

Repeat once more. Beathing in, and out. Now, allow your breath to return to its natural slow and steady rhythm. Just enjoy this sensation. This moment, just for you. Allow yourself to receive this care and attention. You deserve this time to be committed to simply yourself. Allow yourself to enjoy the feelings of relaxation.

Bring your attention to your breath now, how the air flows through your nose into the lungs. Feel as it moves in, expanding the walls of your chest, and then as it is released and relaxed, before your chest contracts once again.

Now, release all expectations. Remove any expectations for this meditation, don't expect certain things to occur, or an insight to come to you. Simply allow yourself to be present in this moment. You aren't needed anywhere else, but here. There is nothing you need to do now. Productiveness isn't needed right now. There is nothing else your mind needs to think about. If you find your mind does wander, bringing about random thoughts, that's okay. Just notice and acknowledge each thought briefly, before allowing it to pass. These thoughts and internal chatter will begin to fade into the background, becoming less and less noticeable. Don't engage and let these thoughts bother you. Part of your minds role is producing thoughts, and this function can't always be turned of immediatly. All you require is some time and patience, so your mind can become experianced in relaxation and having some free time to remain off duty.

Now, imagine you find yourself walking up towards the top of a hill. The day is beautiful with a clear blue sky and the sun beams down on you. The air is pleasantly warm, yet refreshingly cool. You reach the top of the hill. This place is enchanting. As you gaze into the horizon, you feel calmed by the high mountains and the winding, glittering river, down in the valley. White fluffy clouds appear sparingly in the sky, gently floating along with the soft breeze.

Now, you lie-down, onto the thick bed of green grass beneath you. It is soft and soothes your entire body. Right here, you are completely safe and free. The air from the mountains is so pure and refreshing. Take a deep breath in, allowing it to spread through your entire body. Exhale slowly.

As you lay on the soft, soothing grass, bring your focus to your body. Allow it to slip into relaxation completely. Firstly, bring attention to your toes and feet. Relax them and let them drift open slightly, up towards the sky. Feel as the grass gently tickles your feet. Now moving to your ankles, relax them. Let your calfs relax too. Move slowly upward, and relax your knees and thigh muscles. Feel the backside of your thighs, and how they feel against the grass beneath you. As you exhale, your muscles become heavier and looser. Relax your glutes, noticing again how they feel against the ground. Let your hips loosen and relax.

Your hands lay beside your body, straight and open to the sky above. Focus intentently on each finger, relaxing them one by one. Notice how they begin to softly tingle as they do so. Move to your palms now, relax them. Release all the tension you carry from your hands. Whatever you find yourself holding onto, let it go now. Simply open your palms up to the sky and allow any tension to exit. Your hands serve you all day long, they do so much for you. They deserve this relaxation. Let go of everything, from your hands. Now you feel the soft breeze on your palms. You have created a space for new energy to flow through you, energy that will serve all your true intentions. Relax your wrists and forearms. Feel the gentle touch of the grass under them now. Relax your elbows, notice how they become more loose and flexible. Release all tension from your arms and feel all the muscles in your arms as they soften.

Bring your focus your stomach. Notice how it easily expands as you inhale, just like a balloon, before contracting with your exhale. Allow your chest to relax. Feel your ribcage as it gently sits at rest.

Now it's time to relax your back. Notice how the ground feels against your back, the grass supporting it. Focus on each and every vertebrae starting from the base of your spine to your head. Take your time, making sure every single part is relaxed. Notice as the muscles in your back relax and loosen now too. Imagine your breath flowing in through your spine, before being released back out through it. Relaxing your back as you exhale.

Move to your shoulders, let them relax, loosen, and release. Notice as the softly move down from your ears, resting neutrally where's natural. Often, the weight of all the worries and stress is held on our shoulders. We aren't aware of this weight until it's released, making us feel lighter and more free.

Relax your neck and your throat. Relax the back of your head. Allow the soft green grass to support them comfortably like a pillow.

Listen to breeze as it rustles through the grass and trees. Hear the soothing song from the birds and insects in the grass. Now, allow your ears to relax. Relax your forehead and brows. Release all tension from your eyebrows and allow every tiny muscle around your eyes to relax. Calm your eyes letting them sink into your head, completely relaxed and at rest. Relax your cheeks and lips. Relax your jaw and even your tongue. Allow every part of your face to rest where is natural, rather than being held in any position.

Bring you attention to the surface of your body. Let your skin relax, visualizing how it becomes refreshed and re-energized now.

Now, focus internally. Visualize your internal organs as they relax. How every system inside you, every organ, every cell comes to rest and relax. Feel yourself internally gain fresh new energy and rejuvenate.

Your whole body is relaxed now.

Notice again how the grass feels under your body. You feel completely supported and grounded. You appreciate this grass and give it thanks for supporting and holding you now. Smile, as you enjoy this moment, the ground and the relaxation it brings to you. You thank yourself, for the gift of this moment and the care your body, mind and spirit have received. This relaxation is an invaluable gift, what your body craves most. By receiving this relaxation, your body will show its thanks by performing and serving you even better.

Right now you feel strongly grounded, yet as if your floating on the soft grass beneath you. It's time to release all the extra weight you've been carrying, any hard, dark emotions and thoughts let them go, into the ground beneath you. Imagine them as a dark sand, pouring out your body, onto the ground. Think of any worries or hard feeling you have and tell them: "I'm letting you go now. I'm devolving you to the ground. You don't serve me." Repeat this as many times as you wish, for every negative thought or emotion, and for you want to get rid of.

It's time to relax your mind now. You may find thoughts come and go. This is perfectly normal. When your relaxed, the mind notices them but lets them quickly pass by. Don't engage in them, right now is not the time to analyze these thoughts and emotions, getting caught in them. Don't follow any thought, but rather observe from a distance. Your mind is so used to working all the time, following and trusting in every thought that arises. So not engaging in them may be completely new and strange for you. Now you're at rest you can see these thoughts for what they truly are, just thoughts. These can so easily be pushed away, as they aren't truth, but simply creations of your mind.

Now, you look up at the blue sky above you. It's a perfect sunny day. The sky is almost clear, although scattered with fluffy clouds. Some of these clouds are greyish as they carry rain. You understand the meaning of these clouds - they represent your thoughts. The fluffy white clouds are your positive thoughts, the clear neutral ones are thoughts about what you need to do, where to go, the different ideas that pop up in your mind. Whereas the greyish clouds filled with rain represent your negative, difficult thoughts, worries, and fears.

You can feel a fresh breeze ripple through your hair. Althought this breeze is gentle down here, up high in the sky this wind moves these clouds. The wind moves them along so each slowly disappears from view. As these clouds float away, they carry your thoughts with them. One by one, they disappear, the sky remaining a clear blue, just like your mind as it fills with clarity. Your mind is calm, resting, and you enjoy the silence of your inner mental space and the clear blue sky.

Now, you get up, standing on the soft green grass you gaze into the distance from the hill. The gentle breeze has now gained strength from the mountains around you and is now a fresh wind. It's a pleasant cold, that brings you the pure mountain air. Inhale deeply. Fill your lungs with this pure and refreshing energy. Notice if any tension and unwanted emotions remain, release them with your exhale. Whatever you don't need anymore, let it go, taken by the cleansing wind. Any tension and negativity that wasn't sent to the ground earlier, is now washed away by the wind. Any thoughts and belief that no longer serve you, let them go into the wind too. Any guilt, anger, fear, jealousy, any sour emotions, let them be taken by the wind. Floating away until they no longer remain.

The wind grows stronger now. It no longer blows gently past you, but completely through you. The wind blows through your clothes, your skin, through all your tissues and bones. All you carry that doesn't serve you, the wind takes as it flurries through you. You enjoy the sensation as the cool wind cleanses you. Allow yourself to fully experience this, trusting in the winds power and intentions. Enjoy the feeling as the pure, cool wind cleanses your entire being, leaving you feel filled with energy and clarity.

Inhale, visualizing refreshing energy fill your lungs. Exhale, releasing all mental and physical strain. It's time to get rid of any negative residue - the wind will carry it away. This time is for only you, to become reenergized and be mentally and physically cleansed, so that fresh energy, thoughts, and ideas can easily flow in.

Repeat what I say, mentally or out loud: "I inhale health."

"I breathe out," and say anything you want to release.

"I inhale prosperity."

"I breathe out," and again repeat what you want to let go.

Repeat this a few times, for everything you want to be released and cleansed by the wind.

Feel the wind flowing in and around you. Enjoy this flow and become a part of it. Simply experience this for a while.

Eventually, as the wind has cleansed all it need to, it drops back to a soft breeze. You are completely healed and cleansed now. You feel lighter, calm and energized. Your body is entirely relaxed and renewed. Your mind is fresh and clear, just like the cloudless sky.

Whenever you feel ready to leave this meditation, softly open your eyes. Return to your day and its activities, or drift off to sleep.

Whenever you are in need of being completely cleansed and reenergized, or just relaxed, you can return. The soft grass on the hill, the blue sky, the surrounding mountains, and the cleansing wind remain here for your return.

Guided Meditation for Relaxation 2

Welcome to this meditation that will assist you in reaching a deeper level of relaxation for both your body and mind.

Relaxation is a powerful tool, yet most of us don't allow ourselves the opportunity for relaxation in our usual daily lives. Often we walk through life with heavy shoulders and our bodies filled with tension. The weight of tension we carry daily can only make itself known when we relax, so often we aren't aware of how much better we can perform without it.

When we relax, so much good can happen. With regular relaxation our body can be free of any tension. Throughout our day our minds are in in constant use, so need a break once in a while to refresh. When tense, new energy and prosperity struggles to flow into our life. Through relaxation, this pathway of new energy can be opened so it can flow through us, benefiting our body and mind, in all aspects of life.

Providing yourself time for relaxation is one of the best forms of self-care. Allowing yourself this time enables you to take care of yourself, and therefore care for others too. So feel no guilt for taking the time to follow this meditation, as it is not only your highest good but also the highest good for those around you.

This time is just for you. You deserve it all. No matter what else you may need to do, allowing yourself relaxation is the best thing you can do. As this will only increase your productivity and ability to perform at your best. So, allow yourself to enjoy these precious moments.

I invite you to follow my guidance now.

Choose any place and any time of a day or night when you know you won't be disturbed. Get yourself into a comfortable position, sitting or lying down. Allow yourself to be a pleasant temperature, so use a blanket to get warm if you need.

Take a few moments to prepare for this journey by calming yourself and slowing down. Using your stomach, take a few deep breaths. As you exhale, feel your body relax more and more.

Now, imagine you are on a beautiful beach. The sun above is sowly going in, leaving a beautiful sunset. You are walk barefoot along the sand, feeling as it slinks through your toes. It's warm, soft, and feels like a gentle massage.

The warm air has a fresh seaside smell. A salty breeze brushes your face. Breathe in and let this refreshing air fill your lungs.

Now slowly breathe out.

Repeat this once again.

Inhale.

Slowly exhale.

For now, you've decided you have had enough of walking and its time to rest.

You sit or lie down on the soft sand. Now the sun is beginning to set, the sand is left with a beautiful, golden shine. It's smooth, and it shapes to support your body. You get comfortable with it, and it provides you with a soothing warmth.

You enjoy the sounds of the waves as they roll in. This is one of the most relaxing sounds in the world. The rush as the waves curl over shore, dissolving into foam.

Breathe in, deeply with your belly, and simply focus on the sounds of the waves. Release any urges to do anything, and any thoughts of your day. Right now, there is nothing else you should be doing. Just enjoy the soft touch of the sand as it supports you, how it feels under your back, legs and your hands. Notice how the warm, soothing sand cradles your head like a pillow. Breathe in with your stomach, and listen to the sounds of the sea.

Now, shift your focus to your breath. Inhale counting to four. One, two, three, four.

Hold it inside to the count of three. One, two, three.

Exhale, counting to seven. One, two, three, four, five, six, seven.

Now repeat this process again.

Inhale, counting to four. One, two, three, four.

Hold for three. One, two, three.

Exhale, for seven. One, two, three, four, five, six, seven.

Now repeat once more.

Inhale, counting to four.

Hold, counting to three.

Exhale, counting to seven.

Now, let your breathing return to its natural rhythm.

Bring your attention to your body. Notice how your body feels right now. Does it feel heavy or tense? Notice where you hold any tension in your body.

Your body does so much for you. It serves you every day in all activities and holds your beautiful soul. Take a moment to give it thanks for doing just that.

Now, we will work on relaxing the whole body, part by part.

Starting from your head, notice your forehead and eyebrows now, Inhale, as you do so scrunching them so they're tense. Exhale, allowing them to relax completely.

Now notice all the tiny muscles in your face, around your eyes, your cheek, your lips. Inhale, tensing them all. Then exhale, releasing and relaxing all these muscles too. Enjoy the rest your eyes are receiving now.

Observe any tension in the back of the head. Relax it all.

Tense your neck now. Then, count back from ten, gradually relaxing your neck and your thoat. Notice your tense shoulders and drop them down from your ears, relaxed.

Stretch your back out, so each section stands tall. With your exhale, release your back so it sits neutrally where's natural. As you slowly relax each muscle, imagine as if your whole back is recieving a calming, warm massage. Notice as you focus on each muscle, it become soothingly warm.

Take a deep breathe in, filling your lungs with refreshinga air. Breathe out, allowing your lungs to completely relax.

Bring your awareness to your abdominals. Notice how your stomach is relaxed, simply following the rhythm of your breath, epanding and contracting as you need. Feel the peace of right here.

Shift your focus to your hands. Feel the warm, soft sand beneath them. Take a moment to give thanks for your hands. For they serve you everyday, for so many years already. Stretch and extend your fingers, exhale and relax them. Relax your palms, opening them to the sky above. Tense all the muscles in your whole arm and hands now, then release them – your wrists, forearms, elbows, all the way to your shoulder.

Squeeze your glute and thighs. Exhale, release and relax. Allow them to relax your hip and pelvic area too.

Now, tense your knees and calf muscles, rasing your toes up as you do so. Allow them to tighten as much as you can, then, as you breathe out loosen them completely. Relax your whole legs now, right from your hip to your knees, and from your knees to your ankles.

Lastly, inhale tensing your feet. Then exhale, relaing them. Relax your toes, your heels, your whole foot.

Your whole body is completely relaxed now.

Enjoy the calming sensations you feel in your body right now. Feel the warm soothing rays as they set on your skin, and the soft sand that cushions your body beneath you.

Now remaining on the beach, open your eyes. You get up from the warm sand, stretching your muscles as you stand. You feel energized and refreshed.

You feel drawn to the sea, and wish to bathe in its cool, salty waters. You know this would be a wonderful healing and relaxing experiance. The sea surface sparkles under the gentle evening light. As you step into the water, imagine a golden, healing liquid enter through your feet, slowly spreading up through your legs to the rest of your body. Now your in the water neck deep, your whole body full of this glistening, golden liquid. All you don't want, any old, negative energy drains out of you, into the deep blue. This leaves room for new refreshing energy to enter within you. You dive head first into the cool water, as you do so thoughts and worries that make residence in your mind, flows out into the water. Your mind is clear and rejuvenated.

Now, you let yourself float calmly on the waters surface. You feel light and full of clarity as the sea completely supports your weight. Enjoy this deeper state of relaxation you feel right now.

When you feel ready, swim back to the beach. You return to the soft, glistening sand and wrapp yourself in a huge, soft towel. Feel its comforting warmth.

You will know when the meditation is finished, as your body and mind will feel completely relaxed, re-energized, and renewed. You will feel ready to return to your daily activities or fall asleep.

So, whenever you're ready, gently open your eyes and enjoy your day. Or, if you want, drift off to deep slumber, and have nice dreams.

Guided Meditation for Overcoming Insomnia

Welcome to the guided meditation for overcoming insomnia. If you have trouble falling asleep from time to time or seemingly everynight, this meditation is for you.

Use it in the evening before you intend to sleep. Get into your bed, and make yourself comfortable. Lie however you wish, on your back, side or stomach, whatevers most comfortable. Just listen to my voice, and allow it to guide you to a state of deep relaxation, from where you can easily drift off to sleep.

Don't worry if you fall asleep mid-way through the meditation, as my voice and guidance will still impact the subconscious mind helping you not only fall asleep easier, but also remain alseep throughout the night. I will guide you to a deeper slumber, so you will finally get a proper, productive nights rest.

Falling asleep and remaining in sleep during the whole night is a habit. Like any habit, time and practice are required for it to be formed. You can use this meditation every night, whilst you form a habit of good sleep and overcome your insomnia.

After a night of deep sleep, you will be completely rested, and be able to wake up refreshed and renewed.

You may struggle to fall asleep because you're overthinking, allowing thoughts to concern you and forming an endless to-do list. If you resonate, I would suggest pausing this right now, and writing it all down before you continue. Whatever it is, put it aside, onto paper and out your busy mind. You will deal with it tomorrow. Now, this time is for you. For relaxation, rest and to recharge.

So, shift your focus to this moment, the soft, comfortable bed you find yourself on, and to here and now. Simply relax and listen to my voice, there is nothing else you need to do. You will be guided into a perfect sleep.

Inhale deeply, and hold it to the count of three. Then, release.

Repeat this again – Inhale deeply, hold counting to three. One, two, three. Then exhale.

Now, repeat once more - breathe in, hold to the count of three. Then, breathe out.

Let your breathing drop back to its natural pattern. Don't force it into a rythm that unatural; just do what's pleasant for you.

With each exhale, let your body become lose and more relaxed.

Now, observe your thoughts as they flow by. A busy mind means your constantly preoocupied by different thoughts as they rise up like bubbles all the time. Your mind deserves a rest. Realize they are just thoughts. They are not your thoughts, but a product of a busy mind. Exhale, your mind is slowing now. Fewer and fewer thoughts arise now as your mind becomes slower and more relaxed.

Since a busy mind is used to working at all times, simply banishing thoughts entirely is not an option. But what you can do is to focus on something else. By occupying your mind with certain mindful thoughts, you can push away any unwanted ones.

So, to help keep you grounded, bring awareness to how your body feels and its physical sensations.

Become mindful of how it feels. Feel how the bed underneath you supports your bodys weight. Feel the soft, soothing warmth. Feel the weight of your bed covers, your temperature and the temperature around you. Feel the steady rhythm of your heartbeat. Listen to the sound of your breath. Feel how the cool air enters through your nose, filling your lungs. Observe how your stomach expands as you inhale.

Acknowledge any tension that exists in your body currently. Imagine it rising to the surface of your body allowing you to release it all.

Right now, there is so much in your body and surroundings that you can become aware of. Being present and mindful allows you to vacate your busy mind.

The most effective way to relax your body and mind is by placing your focus with your breath. Notice as you do so, that this also provides you with relaxing effects.

You may find completely random thoughts may arise in your mind, simply acknowledge their existance before allowing them to pass. Return your attention back to your body maintaining focus on your breath. Continue to inhale and exhale, observing how the air flows through your body and back out again.

Your breath alone will help you remain easily and naturally, calm and relaxed, so you can gradually fall asleep.

Now I invite you to use your imagination. Feel free to do so with your eyes opened or closed. It's up to you.

Visualize your mind as a spinning wheel. It spins around at a fast speed, just like your busy mind. Now, allow it to gradually slow down, more and more.

Now it's turning very slowly, it's barely moving. Time has slowed down, it's no longer something that controls you. Thoughts appear less often, they have slowed with it. You are relaxed. Your mind is calm and clear.

Your eyes begin to tire and struggle to watch the wheel as it slowly turns. They need rest. Now, push this image further and further away. It become smaller and smaller, further into your clear dark mind until it is barely even a distant dot.

Now, as you lay completly calmly you imagine you're lying under the shade of a huge tree on some soft grass. Your a shepherd and it's a lazy, warm afternoon. The evening draws nearer and you need to round up all your sheep before night falls. The sun begins to set, and you have fifty sheep to collect under the lavish orange sky. You start to count the sheep as you collect them one by one across the large field. One, two, three, four, five, six, seven, eight, nine, ten, eleven, twelve... Count further. Count until all of your sheep are safetly collected and together. You take them to their inclosure, readying them for a sleep filled night.

You are tired from your long day, so you lie on the grass once again. You're snuggling into a warm and comfortable sleeping bag. Tonight your going to sleep outdoors, accompanied by your sheep and the stars above. You gaze at the glistening stars, and think about those who will be born this very night, under these very stars. You start to give names to the stars and the children who may be born under them. The first one is Grace, and the second one is Jake, the third one is Charlie, the fourth is James, the fifth is Megan, the sixth is Rachael, the seventh is Mathew, the eighth is Helen, the ninth is Alex, the tenth is Terry... and so on. You made up ten names. Then ten more. You continue to give names to the stars and children that are going to be born until you feel so tired you struggle to think of anymore. You doze off and fall into deep, deep sleep. You will sleep the whole night undisturbed, and, when you wake in the morning, you will feel great, refreshed, and ready for a completely new day.

Guided Meditation for Overcoming Depression

Welcome to this meditation for overcoming depression.

The use of meditation for healing depression have been researched, and the techniques used in this meditation are evidence-based. So trust in this meditation whenever you are in need of relief from any sour feelings. Using this meditation daily will tremendously help you and your efforts to overcoming depression.

Your mind has become entrapped in a cycle of producing chemicals, that make you feel bad. You need to work on reversing this process, creating a habit of producing them feel-good chemicals that will make you feel great. This meditation will guide you on how to do just that. So, the goal of this meditation is to simply make you feel good. This is the soul focus of right now. Allow yourself to feel the positive effects of this meditation, you mind may show resistance to this at first, but that is because you are breaking a habit of negative thinking. With the guidance of meditation, you will build a new habit of feeling good, helping to reverse your current negative cycle of thinking. Building a new habit takes practise and time, so try to practise this meditation daily before you sleep. Enjoy the little steps you are making towards a better daily life. As you start to do small things that make you feel good, you build the foundations for a joyful, happy life.

Now, prepare yourself for relaxation. Make sure your are comfortable. Take a deep breath in and out, and relax. Simply focus on your breath right now, as we work on relaxing your entire body.

Inhale, as you do so count to four. One, two, three, four.

Exhale, counting to six while you relax your feet. One, two, three, four, five, six.

Take another deep breath, counting to four. One, two, three, four.

Release this breath, counting to six, now, relaxing your lower legs. One, two, three, four, five, six.

Inhale again, counting to four. One, two, three, four.

Exhale, until you reach six, releasing all tension from your thighs. One, two, three, four, five, six.

Take a deep breath, to the count of four.

Breathe out, relaxing your glutes, hips, and pelvic area, to the count of six.

Count to four, as you inhale.

Exhale, relaxing your fingers and palms, while you count to six.

Take another breath, to the count of four.

Breathe out, counting to six, relaxing your forearms as you do so.

Inhale deeply, until you reach the count of four.

Exhale, reaching the number six, and relaxing your elbows.

Breathe in, counting to four.

Breathe out, to the count of six, allowing the air to carry away any tension from your upper arms.

Take a breath, to the count of four, expanding your stomach.

Exhale, to the count of six, noticing how your belly contracts. Allow it to relax now.

Breathe in, counting to four.

Breathe out, to the count of six, allowing your chest to relax.

Take another deep breath, continuing to count to four.

Releasing this air, counting to six, and relaxing your whole back. Remove any hold you have over your back allowing it to sit where's natural.

Now breathe in again, to the count of four.

Breathe out, counting to six, and relaxing your shoulders. You hold lots of weight on your shoulders so repeat this once more.

Inhale, counting to four.

Exhale, to the count of six, and relax.

Breathe in - one, two, three, four.

Breathe out and relax your neck and throat - one, two, three, four, five, six.

Inhale, to the count of four.

Exhale, counting to six, and relax even the smallest muscles in your face. One, two, three, four, five, six.

You feel relaxed. Your entire body has been cleansed by the refreshing air you breathe.

Now move your attention to your mind, and the thoughts that inhabit it currently. Take a deep breath in and release, allowing them to disappear alongside your breath. Release everything that doesn't serve your true intentions. Don't be afraid to let go, you don't need these negative thoughts anymore. Let them fade away and disappear. Allow your mind to slow. Now your mind has quietened somewhat, pay attention to the thoughts that remain. Acknowledge their prescence, but continue to let your mind slow. Take a deep breath, again. Exhale, releasing your remaining thoughts with your breath again. Your mind is clear and relaxed. You feel good, completely calm and at peace. Tell yourself: I feel good and I need no reason to feel good.

Inhale deeply, Exhale. Mentally tell yourself: I feel great. But also believe it.

Breathe in and breathe out, again.

Bring your awareness to your body, noticing how it feels and any tension in it. Inhale, as you do so, allowing this tension to collect at one concentrated point inside of you. Exhale, and let it out. Release all tension along with your breath. Let it go. As you release, you start to feel even better. Breathe in and breathe out. Tell yourself again: I feel great.

Now, focus on any pain that continues to hide, deep in your body. Take a deep breath in, and exhale, releasing all that pain. You don't need pain. You are in search of feeling great. Believe it as you tell yourself: I feel great.

Do you notice any suffering in your body? It might be old self-inflicted suffering or from the present. Whatever the suffering, bring it to the surface with your inhale. Exhale now, releasing all suffering outside, along with the breath. Let it all go. Give yourself permission to feel great.

Your body is relaxed. Your mind filled with clarity and peace. You feel great.

Notice the connection you have between your body and mind. How they work together and feel together. Truely visualize this connection. Imagine your brain as it produces chemicals that invoke feelings of happiness and joy. They feel amazing. Feel those vibrations in your mind as they make you feel wonderful in every way, and every part of you. Visualize and truely see those signals as they spread from your brain to every inch of your body.

Breathe in, and out.

Tell yourself mentally or out loud: I feel good. I feel amazing.

Your subconscious mind doesn't have the ability to distinguish between true and false. It simply believes what you tell it. So, feed your subconscious mind positivity, which will allow you to build new patterns of thinking that will work for your highest good. Feel the small pulses which begin in your brain, and travel through your whole body, spreading wonderful emotions. Enjoy these sensations and feelings your mind provides you with. Notice how the positive emotions become stronger and more prevelant as you begin to feel better and better. You deserve to feel amazing; you don't need any reasons for that. Take this time for just you, to feel great for no reason. The feelings of positivity begin to make make their pathway in your body stronger and more powerful. Allow yourself to enjoy it. Inhale. Exhale. Repeat to yourself: I feel good. I feel amazing. I am enjoying this moment.

Now, take the time to recall all you are grateful for, no matter the size and significance. Focus on all your blessings now, all that that brings you joy, all those people who bring happiness into your life, and all the joy you give to others. Feel gratitude as it spreads through you, and your subconscious, soaking it all up. Enjoy this emotion as your every cell absorbs it, remaining with it for as long as you wish. Your body and mind is filled with pure goodness right now.

As you sink into a relaxing slumber or a deep state of peace, enjoy those affirmations:

I am filled with joy.

I feel great.

Happiness fills my every cell.

I am loved.

I love myself.

I am grateful for every last blessing.

I am strong and powerful.

I am full of energy.

I see the good as it finds me.

I am complete and enough.

I deserve to feel loved and great.

My life is meaningful and I create my own purpose.

I create a better life for myself and those I love.

Gratefulness fills me.

I am thankful for all the amazing people in my life.

I am thankful for everything I encounter, and what lessons I have learned.

Thank you.

I feel amazing.

I feel valued.

Joy fills me.

Happiness fills me.

I am full of love. Love for myself, love for everything and everyone.

I am grateful.

I am full of a strong, powerful energy.

I see the good in all I encounter.

I am complete and enough.

I deserve to feel loved and great.

My life is meaningful and I create my own purpose.

I create a better life for myself and those I love.

Gratefulness fills me.

I am thankful for all the amazing people in my life.

Thank you. Thank you. Thank you.

Guided Meditation for Overcoming Depression 2

Welcome to this meditation, for escaping the cycle of depression, for those who have become entrapped by it.

People who don't understand depression and those who suffer from it, often think it is the same as being sad or unmotivated. These same people may even advise you to simply shake it off or deal with it. In reality, the truth is very different. Everyone has tough days from time to time. But, those who suffer from depression, can feel that every day is never-ending and horrid. That nothing is fulfilling anymore, and the whole world seems to have lost its colour.

In this meditation, I'll try to bring back some light and colour back into your life. We will work on noticing even the smallest positive side to all things. This may be hard, as your brain is so used to playing tricks on you. But with time, practice and consistency, you can train your mind to produce those substances that make you feel good once again. Allowing you to free yourself from a cycle of pain and negativity.

So, take a deep breath in, counting to four. One, two, three, four.

Breathe out, counting to eight. One, two, three, four, five, six, seven, eight.

Again repeat, breathing in, to four. One, two, three, four.

And breathe out, counting: one, two, three, four, five, six, seven, eight.

Now, take a deep breathe in, and hold your breath to the counting down to three - three, two, one. Breathe out, saying to yourself, "relax."

Again, breathe in, and hold - three, two, one. Exhale and "relax."

You are free to relax now; you are completely safe.

Now shift your focus to how you feel right now. Is there any tension within you? Where are you holding this tension? Notice any. It may be hiding in your neck, your shoulders, your toes, or maybe your jaw? Do you notice any emotions that fill you? Do you feel nervous, as if butterflies flutter in your stomach? Relax those parts. Take a moment to scan your whole body, start from the very top of your head, down to the tips of your toes. Notice where you hold tension in your body. Focus on those parts, allowing this tension to loosen and those parts to relax.

Perhaps your mind is filled with thoughts passing through right now. Let them all go, just as quickly as they entered. Your thoughts are just your minds doing. You don't always have to believe and follow each one. They hold no power over you, you are in control and in complete power. Just allow them to pass by, like trains as they pass a station

While we work on reversing your typical cycle of thinking, so you can see the good side of things. You mind will try to play tricks on you, as it is used to focusing solely on negativity. Time is required to rewire your brain to rewire and work properly again, so trust in the process. It is a matter of brain chemistry, but you can do a lot to ensure you gain back control, over your mind.

Now, imagine your are sat on the edge of a chair in an empty room. Your sat next to a suitcase of your stuff, and are waiting for a taxi to come and pick you up. You are ready and prepared for a journey.

Now, as you wait for a cab to come, you use this time to close your eyes and think about the different things and circumstances that have affected you recently, and what has brought you here. What does your current life look like? What has made you become seperate from your old self?

Take a moment to congratulate yourself, for truely seeing things for what they are. You have taken a huge step towards your healing and growth.

Imagine you open your eyes now. Everything makes sense now. You are filled with clarity, and can see the present clearly, without feeling the need to shift to the past and future at any point. You are aware of exactly what you need to let go. You understand that sometimes to move foward we need to let go of things first.

Your taxi is now outside, ready for you. You pick up your luggage, closing the front door behind you as you make your way to the vehicle. The driver takes your suitcases, placing them in the boot. He opens the door for you, and you're sat on the backseat. The driver starts the engine and begins to move away from the house. You look from the window, seeing your life for what it is. You observe all you don't like in your current life, it all seems greyish and tiring. You about the break you crave from it all. You know when you return your perspective will be different.

Now you have reached the train station. The kind driver smiles, and wishes you a nice holiday. You stand on the platform and await the trains arrival.

Finally the train is here. You get on and find yourself in a large carrige on your own. You take a seat and get comfortable, ready for a long ride ahead. The train departs from the station, the world outside the window looks different now. There is green all around you, beautiful green trees, fields, hills and mountains in the distance. The further you move away, the more different things look. You think about possibilities and changes. Everything can change, and there are almost limitless possibilities. Your typical plain, grey sights become green and alive. Change can be scary, but usually only brings about good things. Life is in constant change.

Now, your eyes begin to feel heavy, and you start to doze off. Feel free to take a nap if you wish. There is no where else you need to be right now, nothing else you should be doing. You have time. So rest and relax.

The train slows, and the doors open. It has arrived at the station you've been waiting for. You step off the train and find your new driver, that patiently waits for you with your name on a card. He smiles, taking you to a luxurious limousine, holding its door open for you. The seat is soft and comfortable. You feel safe. Outside, you watch as the world flows by, it's colorful and vibrant.

The taxi pulls in, into an airport for private jets. Your kind driver helps get you and your luggage onto the plane. You take a seat and make yourself comfortable, ready for your journey ahead. The pilot and a stewardess greet you with a smile. You feel welcomed and completely relaxed. The airplane leaves the ground and glides through the air. As it glides higher and higher, waves of positivity seem to flow through you more easily than before. Now, the ground disappears from sight, just like all you have left behind. You deserve this break. You sink into the chair, relaxed. Here is a comfort zone, nothing bad can happen here. So if you wish, feel free to take a nap.

The flight comes close to finishing. The plane smoothly lands. You have arrived at your destination.

Outside the airport, you look for a new taxi. You notice this place is completely different. The world from here seems so much more vibrant, colouful and the air is filled with an exciting buzz from those around you. You look forward to exploring this place further. But for now, you watch this world as it passes from the window of your taxi.

Finally, you've reached your desired destinataion. A beach stay in a small, pretty cottage. The beach your cottage looks out on is beautiful, with pearl white sand, and the sea like a melted turquoise. You step inside the cottage. Inside everything is just as relaxing and you can still hear the waves as they roll onto the beach. You take you shoes off, and head back outside. Your barefoot feels soothed by the warm soft sand and it feels relaxing to walk along the beach. It seems like such a long time ago, that you felt this relaxed. It feels like being yourself once again.

The day draws to an end, and the sun begins to set. The sky looks magnificent, it's filled with warm fiery colours, when normally it only seems to be filled with greys. You sit comfortably on the sand, and simply take in your surroundings. You notice so many things – the seagulls as they swoop up and down, the sun as it glistens on the water's surface and the water as it trickles from the rocks on the edge of the beach.

You start to feel a relaxing tired wash over you.

You make your way back to the cottage. Inside a a queen-sized bed with a comfy mattress and white sheets, waits patiently for you. You have left all your worries behind, which have been replaced with feelings of peace and serenity. You calmy lay your head down on the soft pillow and begin to fall asleep. Your muscles feel heavy and relaxed. Your mind is clear, with emotions as light as feathers, so you find it easy to drift off into a deep slumber.

When you wake, you will remember this journey and the sense of peace and tranquility it provided you with.

Guided Mindfulness Meditation for Overcoming Anxiety

Welcome to the guided meditation which uses mindfulness for overcoming anxiety. Being mindful simply means being consciously present in a moment, and aware of everything that's going on within and around you.

Today, anxiety is a common issue. Its completely unpleasant and can feel as if you are in danger at all times, although there's nothing that endangers you. Your mind does its best to try and protect you, turning on your "fight or flight,, mode preparing you for danger. Since their is no real danger this state can do more harm to you than good, so your mind is actually what endangers you most. You need to find a way to tell your mind that you are okay, that you are safe and don't need as much protection. To deliver this message to your brain, you need to calm your breathing and body, so your "fight or flight' mechanism can be switched of and your mind can slow, giving up on overprotecting you.

Often, anxiety is caused by the constant racing of our minds. Find comfort in the fact that you aren't alone in this, that many people all over the world search for ways to cope with anxiety. Fortunately you are in luck, as mindfulness can be tremendously helpful here. Since anxiety is a consequence of being mentally present in the future too much, bringing awareness to right here and now can make huge difference to you. Being mindful means you have found that golden point of awareness in the present.

Through your decision to take this time to practise this meditation, and learn more about mindfulness, means you have already taken the first step towards overcoming your anxiety.

During this meditation, our focuses will be to calm and slow the breath, becoming aware of our physical sensations, relaxing the whole body, and remaining consciously present for a while. By paying attention to our physical sensations, we can use it to ground ourselves to the present moment, heping us to stay away from the busy chaos of your mind before relaxation takes over. In turn, relaxation will remind your mind that you are in no danger and no longer needits overprotection.

So, find somewhere you can sit comfortably and quiet for the next forty minutes or so. Placing your body in comfort can put your mind at ease too. So sit or lay down, whatever you find most comfortable. Make sure your wearing loose comfortable clothing, and that you are a perfect temperature for you. Feel free to practise this meditation before sleep, simply prepare yourself for bed as you usually would.

Allow my voice to guide you through this experience, as we move towards achieving complete awareness and presence. Feel free to gently close your eyes, or keep them slightly open, either way try to stay alert for now.

Using your slight vision, or your minds eyes focus on any particular point in front of you. Narrow your focus to exactly this point, and allow everything else to fade away, simply into your surroundings.

Now, gradually allow this point of focus to grow slowly, until your whole background comes into your full field of vision. With awareness, obseve all you can see infront of you. Consciously keep your head at this exact position, and simply observe all in your view. What colours and textures can you see? Remove any judgement you may have about what you see, simply notice the colours, shapes, shades, textures and materials. Notice the tiny details that you would simply look past in everyday life.

Bring your attention to your breathing. Our breath is one of the most simple yet powerful tools for grounding ourselves in the present. Don't attempt to change anything about your breath now. Just notice its natural rythm, its depth and its natural frequency. Listen to its sound. Notice any parts of your body that move with your breath, as if connected to this air as it moves through you.

Now, with intention begin to deepen your inhale and slow down as you exhale.

Breathe in through your nose, counting to four as you do so. One, two, three, four.

Then breathe out, also through the nose, counting to six. One, two, three, four, five, six.

Repeat this process a few time more.

Inhale. One, two, three, four.

Exhale. One, two, three, four, five, six.

Breathing in this way, with exhales longer than inhales, will emphasize to your mind that you are safe to relax. That you are okay and have no need to run or fight. That you can infact rest and relax

Use this time to notice all that you can about your breath.

Pay particular attention to those perfect still moments, the pauses between every breath. Enjoy the sensation as the refreshing air fills your body, before leaving once again. Feel how it flows through you, its pathway from your nostrils, all the way to your lungs, and then back outside again.

Once again, inhale – one, two, three, four. And exhale – one, two, three, four, five, six.

If you find your regular breathing is too shallow, deeper, or you can't seem to reach those numbers, don't force it. Just try to make your exhales longer than your inhales.

As you find so often, thoughts may be flying through your mind. Don't allow these thoughts to bother you, this is perfectly normal. You mind is used to being busy, in constant worry. Just allow these thoughts to pass through, without your engagement. Imagine these thoughts and emotions as ballons in the sky, floating peacefully away. As your mind slows, fewer ballons float, their speed becoming slower and slower.

Bring your awareness to the pauses between each breath, notice your mind have similar pauses between each thought. Mentally link the two together. Allow yourself to remain in this gap between breaths and thoughts. Enjoy the peacefulness of this space, and rest here. If your mind still wanders away with these thoughts, come back to your breath and the gap between each.

Now, broaden your awareness to the physical sensations of your body.

Feel where your body connects to the surface beneath you. You may feel this line of connection is blurred, or it may feel as if a pressure or warmth. Feel your feet on this surface, or how your back feels against the chair. If you are lying, notice how the surface touches your entire back, legs and arms. Notice this surfaces temprature, its texture and what colour it feels like. Is it smooth cool, or a soft warm?

Become aware of all your senses now. Sense all you can smell. Focus on any scents you are aware of, and how they make you feel.

Then bring your attention to any sounds that surround you. What can you hear? Perhaps you can hear the gentle rumble of cars outside, the birds as they sing, or the sound of people as they go about their day. Maybe you can hear unique sounds and clicks of your house, and appliances as they're used by other members of the house. Notice the sound of your breath. Acknowledge the rhythm of your heart as it beats gently in your chest. Notice the tiniest of details in the sounds you hear. Around us, there is always so many different sounds; it's just a matter of focus if we notice them.

Begin to bring your attention to your body. Start by observing the surface of your body, your skin. Become aware of all it touches. Feel brush of your hair and clothes against it, how it lays squashed against the covers or the chair you sit on. Notice the temperature of the air that touches your skin, of this space.

Take a deep breath in, filling your stomach with calm, refreshing air. Exhale as slowly as you can, enjoying the sensation as it moves through your body.

Utilize this time, by simply being. Be aware of everything within you and around you, noticing even the smallest of details. Feel the beat of your heart and how your blood is pushed smoothly around your body.

Bring awareness to your body as a whole. Sense its aliveness in all the parts of it, in its upkeep of every system, organ and cell. Your awareness of these sensations, are the most effective tool for grounding you to the present, right now.

Inhale deeply, allowing your chest to expand thoroughly, so your stomach expands like a ballon.

As you exhale, focus on your hands, fingers, and palms. Sense the aliveness in those areas, their warmth, or slight tingling. An urge to move your fingers or hands slightly may arise, allow yourself to do so. Feel the movement, and enjoy every sensation.

Now, bring awareness to your arms. Notice everything here, your hair outside as it may rise from the cool air, or the warm flow of blood inside. Notice everything in and around your arms from your wrists to your shoulders. Feel the soft touch of the surface on the backside. Becoming so aware of a particular body part means you are completely relaxing that part.

Now shift your focus to your toes and feet. Feel any tingling in your toes, the relaxed sensation of your feet. Then allow this feeling of relaxation to spread up and through to your ankles, and then your inner legs, your knees, and upper legs. Focus on every sensation in your legs – their warmth, the point of touch between the surface and your skin. Acknowledge and enjoy the sense of relaxation in your hips, glutes, and pelvic area.

Then continue, moving your awareness up, through to your stomach and then chest. Become aware of how your stomach moves in rythm with your breathing. Feel the air as it flows through you, expanding your stomach and chestwalls, before leaving you feeling refreshed and relaxed as you exhale.

Inhale, to the count of four. One, two, three, four. Exhale, to the count of six. One, two, three, four, five, six.

Repeat this a few times more, focusing your undivided attention to how the air flows through your nose, to your lungs and stomach, before making its way back out of you.

Return your attention to the special stillness between every two breaths. Feel grounded to this space, to right now, and allow yourself to sink deeper into this pause, into peace and relaxation.

Again, if any single thought arises, just visualize it as a colorful balloon and watch as it floats peacefully away. Resist any impulse to follow it. Remain at distance from it, simply appriaciate its colour and how it smoothly drifts away from you. You are not your thoughts, they don't define you, and they have no power over you. Acknowledge them as just thoughts, a product of your mind.

Continue with your gradual scan through your body, this time moving to your back. Feel how it connects to the surface beneath or against it. The sensations your back muscles feel now. Are they loose and relaxed? Or tight and tense? Scan through your back, starting from the lowest point allowing each and every area to become relaxed. Feel where is heaviest and the most hot in your back muscles and your spine, noticing any tension that remains. Give special attention to this area, feeling as this tension slowly melts away and is released.

Now move your awareness to your neck. Feel the weight of the head it supports, and acknowledge all the sensations in your throat.

Bring your total awareness to your entire head. How often do you actually engage your focus here? Now, is the time to give it the care and attention it needs. Become aware of every sensation here. If you have hair, notice its touch on your head. Focus on each and every muscle in your face, are you holding them in a position fueled by tension? If so, let go. Scan your face with your awareness, noticing your eyes and mouth, is there any tension here? If so let go, and feel free to close your eyes now too. Take a deep breath in, and enjoy as the fresh, powerful air flows into your head. Allow this air to completely spread through you, relaxing all your muscles.

Take a few more deep breaths in. As you inhale, allow the air to bring you calmness, peace and relaxation. As you exhale, let go of all that doesn't serve your true intentions. Exhale all that tension, which prevents all the peace, clarity and joy from reaching you. As you do so, feel as your body becomes less ridgid and heavy and more soft and relaxed. Allow your body to sink into the surface beneath you, resting completely supported.

Notice all that surrounds you. Feel the temperature that runs over your skin, on your lips, your palms, your lower legs, everywhere. What sounds drift into your ears now? Take this moment to count every last thing you can hear right now. Picture how each, as they enter your ears.

Now, scan through your body once more, notice anywhere that still seems to be holding onto any tension and anxiety. Take a moment to give these areas special attention. Your body is clearly hinting at something that requires more of your time and care, and finally it will recieve just that. Sometimes, simply giving special attention to a sensation in the body is enough to loosen and remove it. So, bring your attention to these areas which are attempting to tell you something. Just stay with these sensations for a moment. You may find your mind may wander into your old patterns of thinking, if so, gently come back to this moment and stay with the experiance of these sensations.

Inhale deeply. Exhale slowly. Allow each breath to bring you peace and healing, and each exhale to take away all you need to let go.

Each moment right now, is so beneficial for you, so enjoy every last second of this time.

Just envision the healing processes that are occuring in your body right now. Feel as your organs, muscles, bones, your every system and cell is filled with a deep sense of peace and relaxation. Enjoy these feelings in your body as you allow it this time to heal and recharge. This time is for your healing alone.

Inhale calm. Exhale anxiety.

Inhale peace. Exhale tension.

Inhale relaxation. Exhale haste.

You are present and aware of all of this moment right now. This is what it feels like to be mindful. That this moment in time is your only reality. Here there is no such thing as past or future, just now. So if any worries float in your mind now, remain in this moment where they can't bother you. If these worries still bother you, imagine you are holding a big, red balloon. Open your hand, make the decision to let it go. If you still feel worries are lingering in your mind, imagine you are holding a bunch of balloons, all different sizes and colours. Then, let go, allow them all to float away from you, leaving you tied down to nothing anymore. You were the only thing holding these balloons here. You don't them anymore. Worries are just a product of your mind, attempting to keep you stuck in the past or trapped in worry over your future. You don't have to engage in them, and if you ever feel yourself drifting into these thoughts, bring your attention back to your breathing, your surroundings, and into the present.

Once you become completely aware and grounded in the present, anxiety has no place to survive. Instead it is released, away with all the colourful ballons you let go of.

Take another deep breath in again. Fill your chest with cool refreshing air, feeling as peace and calmness spreads from your stomach as you do so. Exhale, and allow every last remianing piece of anxiety, tension and business to be released.

Now listen to these affirmations, repeating them mentally or out loud and allowing them to flow through your entire being:

I am aware of my breath. I'm aware of the air as it move in and out of my body.

I am aware of my body, of its every system, of my steady hearts beat.

I am aware of my fears and anxiety. I'm aware of the pain they bring.

I am aware of the negative thoughts that produce my anxiety.

Now, I am slowing my mind.

I am calming my negative thoughts, displacing my usual anxiety.

I am relaxing my body and mind.

I am letting go of any thoughts that don't serve me. Letting go of fears and concerns.

Each moment here, I am finding more peace.

I am safe.

I am aware of my breath, and release all I don't need with my exhale.

I inhale serenity.

Everything's happening for my higher good.

Everything is in the right place.

I am divinely protected and guided.

Everything will fall into perfect place, when the time is right.

Whatever I need will find me.

Whatever I should know, is revealed to me.

I am calm and relaxed.

I am in peace with this moment, with the world, with life.

The world is a safe place for me.

I am powerful and strong.

I am present and grounded.

I am in perfect balance.

I inhale tranquility. I exhale hot tension.

As you breath, smile at yourself .

I am safe and secure. I give myself permission to be in this peace.

I am good.

Things only improve, getting better and better each day.

I anticipate great things will happen.

I accept my anxiety. It is just my mind trying to protect me. Thank you. But, I don't need you anymore. I am completely safe and well now, so I am letting you go.

Feel as you grow lighter.

I accept all of my emotions as what they are, and allow myself to experience them.

They don't define me. I can observe them whilst remaining calm.

I am healingand growing all the time.

My body and mind live together in a healthy harmony.

I allow myself to remain in peace.

I feel rejuvenated, as if reborn.

I feel wellness flow through my whole body, in each and every cell.

I am filled with a new positive energy.

I allow myself to rest in this comfort and peace.

I enjoy this soft tranquility and gentleness.

I enjoy being in this completely relaxed state, free from any anxiety.

You can start over, becoming aware of your presence as many times as you need.

In your everyday life outside meditation, look for patterns and situations where you find yourself rushing. Then, intentionally slow down, remind yourself to completely experience life fully. When we slow down, remaing with our sensations, we become aware of so much more, experiancing life fully. So, allow yourself to slow down, remain in the gap between breaths more and savour life. When you can quiet the noise in your head, you are able to see, hear and feel things with clarity, opening you up to everything around you.

Now, whenever you feel ready, gently open your eyes, stretch yourself, get up, and move on with your daily activities, try to remain slow and open to experiancing life at its fullest.

Guided Meditation For Overcoming Depression

Welcome to this meditation which aims to help in the management of depression and depressive moods.

Here, you'll engage your focus on your breath and learning how to look at your thoughts and feelings in a new way, from a new perspective.

Immediatly after this meditation you may feel more hopeful and positive, but with repeated use, you may notice feelings of depression appear less frequently. With a continued habit of mediation, you may even find yourself acting and feeling as your old self would.

This meditation can be done anywhere and anytime you wish, or whenever you may feel you need an extra boost to help manage your depression. Either way, it's best to choose a time a place you know you won't be disturbed, where you are able to close your eyes and just relax.

To begin, simply get yourself into a comfortable position. Feel free to lie down, sit on a chair or sit on the floor with your legs crossed in front of your. Its up to you, just keep your back straight and make sure your comfortabe.

Ensure your clothes are comfortable, so feel free to loosen all the restrictive pieces such as belts so you can sit softly and free. Turn off any ringers and notifications, so you won't become distracted and disturbed.

Place hands on your lap or your knees, palms facing up. If you are lying, let them straighten next to your body.

Prepare youself for relaxation, so if possible, close your eyes readying you for peace to enter.

Shift your focus to your breath. Take a few deep breaths in now. Breathe in slowly and deeply from your stomach. Connect to your breath, feeling as the cool, fresh air enters your nostrils. Notice the movement of your belly as it moves with your inhales and exhales.

Now, release any control you have over your breath, allowing it to return to its natural rhythm.

Notice every last sensation in your body. Become aware of your posture, how you hold your entire body and every part, sensing all there is to sense.

Allow your breath to flow in its natural slow and steady rhythm.

Depression is universal, a universal experiance for all humans everywhere. It affects everything - our body, the way we think and feel, all aspects of life. Depression brings along a whole host of negative thoughts and feelings that can be hard to escape from. Positivity is so much harder to find, and you may find yourself losing any interest in life. Depression can be a natural reaction to certain things life throws at you, such a loss. On the other hand, depression can seem to arise with no real cause. Either way, there is nothing wrong with you. Your thoughts and emotions are not abnormal. Although they aren't enjoyable at all, depression can actually bring you some good. It can force you to look inward, to search for solutions, reevaluate things and make adjustments, so you begin to learn more about yourself.

From time to time everyone experiances depression. But, falling into depression for too long isn't healthy. Once it has a place within you it has the ability to preserve itself, making you depressed for much longer than you should, and more and more harder to distance yourself from its hold over you.

Fortunately, once you find yourself suffering from depression, it is not a life sentance, and there is infact a solution. This meditation will teach you the techniques that help you cope with depresssion, so you can put them into practise whenever you may need them.

Firstly, you should never suppress, invalidate or ignore any emotions and thoughts. If you fight them, you only give them more power and strength, which can continue to be used against you. You also don't have to figure out the source of these thoughts and feelings, as they won't get you to the root of your problem. So, instead of attempting to force out these unlovable thoughts and emotions, it is much easier and wiser to change your relationship with them. Accept these thoughts, make a small space for them, and don't waste your energy fighting them anymore. Just by providing them this attention, you will be surprised at how easily they lose their power and fade away from you.

Bring your awareness to your body now. Ensure it is comfortable, with a neutral posture, so you can relax, yet stay alert.

Allow your breathing to remain in its natural pattern. You don't need to do anything right now, keep your breaths rhythm and depth the same. Simply breathe as you usually would. Notice the sensations in your nose now. Feel as the cool air enters your nostrils. Now, notice as the air leaves your nostrils, this time notice the airs warmth. Repeat this a few times, just focusing on the cool air as it enters and the hot, bothered air as it leaves your nostrils. Focus your complete attention on your nose now.

Repeat once more—cool air in, warm air out.

Now, fully immerse yourself in your breath and allow yourself to experience it fully. Observe your breath, be curious. Notice its every pathway around your body. Have the experience of breathing and at the same time observe yourself experiancing it.

Removing all judgement and expectations of your breath, notice your breathing's pattern. Does your breath naturally follow a long and deep rhythm? Or a short and shallow one? Notice if your breathing changes or stays the same. Don't try to change it or force it into a particular rhythm, simply leave it be, trusting your body knows best. Remove any beliefs of "how things should be." Instead, accept the things for what they are by just observing them, without trying to take control.

Continue to observe your natural pattern of breathing.

You may find at some point during the meditation, you focus starts to slip and drift off else where. This is perfectly normal, so don't get angry with yourself. We can all become distracted at times, and focusing requires practise and patience.

Distractions always come from one of three sources - your thoughts, senses, or feelings. So when you find yourself distracted, notice it, don't hold onto it and let it go. Once you've acknowledged it, return your focus back to your breath. So with your next distraction, practise this method. Notice, and let go. There is nothing you need to fight and push away, just let it float by.

Whenever your mind begins to wander, notice what's going on in the present moment. Return your focus to you nose, the sensations it feels, the cool air as you inhale and the warm air as you exhale.

You may also feel the urge to name a distraction. This could be mentally telling yourself about how the "alarm is ringing next door," how the "kids are making noise outside," the "traffic," "dog's barking," and so on, about whatever is distracting you. This is expected, but instead try to name just one thing, that's more general and more in connection with what your experiancing right now. So if you either feel your mind "distracting" or "wandering," bring your attention back to your breath. Again, try this for a moment, with the next distraction or mind wandering.

Now, the next time you lose your focus, instead of internally naming these distractions, just notice your focus has been lost and bring it right back to the present. With your next distraction practise this.

Most likely, as you struggle with depression, negative, depressive thoughts and feelings will intrude into this time. These are the thoughts you are trying to escape from the most. The trick here, is to still treat them as any other distraction. This means, rather than following them and attempting to fight them, acknowledge them for what they are and bring your attention back to your breathing. As you start to do this, it will get easier and feel more natural each time, as you already know how to let these thoughts pass. So, try it for a moment. Notice the negative thought as it appears. Gently bring your focus back to your nose and your breath. Let this thought float by easily, without any pushing.

When you seem trapped in a loop of depression and depressive thoughts, your mind is in constant focus on the future or stuck in the past. This means staying in the present, and in the sensations of your current body, helps you stay balanced. Focusing on your breathing is one of the most powerful tools for grounding you in the present, therefore helping you feel balanced. So, for the next few moments, try to remain present with your breath. Follow the airs pathway, as it enters your nostrils, filling your lungs and belly, before leaving you again. Notice even the tiniest of movements that seem to connect with your breath. Feel all the sensations this cool, refreshing air seems to provoke in your body. Be intentionally present, right here, with your next few breaths.

Unfortunatly, depressive thoughts often come in hand with negative thoughts. So you may also feel distracted by feelings of sadness, emptiness, anger, frsutration, and anxiety. Emotions are a combination of thoughts and sensations in your body, which means they are often a product of depression and your minds current cycle of negativity. Acknowledge this, and begin to seperate your negative emotions into the sense in your body and the thoughts behind them. You may feel these negative emotions as an ache somewhere in your body, or a part of you that feels particulary weak and fatigued. Allow yourself to experiance all you feel, without the need to change, solve or eradicate it.

Secondly, notice the thoughts in your mind. Acknowledge the connection between these thoughts and the negative emotions you can sense in your body. Your thoughts have the ability to cause your body to feel a certain way, which is why you experaince the two together as an emotion.

Now, consciously place your attention with the sensations in your body, and not with thought. Allow your attention to rest with any sensations and notice if their instensity changes or remains the same. With your focused attention you may actually find any sensations slowly disappear.

Let emotion and the sensation stay in your body, but gentky bring your awareness back to your breath. Notice how the air flows through your body. Inhale, feel as the cool air enters your nostrils. Exhale, and focus on the warmth of the air as it leaves your nose.

When you choose to follow any distressing thoughts, it gives power to negative feelings, only making them grow stronger. In contrast, when you give your undivided attention and focus to the negative sensations they create in your body, depressive thoughts diminish, making you feel balanced and liberated from this cycle of negativity.

Feel now, as you give your breath and physical sensations your full focus, that you are completely grounded in the present, which seems to provide you with more relief than anything else.

Use this next moment to imagine you are at a train station. Around you, people rush around in all directions pushing and bumping into one another ditracted by their day and not the present moment. You stand still on the edge of the platform, awaiting your train. You notice that everything surrounding you seems grey and dull. Colourless. The faceless people who lack emotion, pace around in their grey suits. The platform itself is a dirty grey, with ugly trains that pull in every so often. You look down and see you are wearing a plain, grey almost uniform, as it lacks shape and character. You also carry a large, heavy, black bag. Your shoulder is sore from its weight, but you can't put it down. You have to carry it wherever you go.

As you stand back and observe this strange lifeless world, random thoughts may arise. If this happens, don't worry- all this mental chatter will pass. So simply acknowledge these thoughts breifly and be gentle with yourself, this is only normal. Let the people and your thoughts pass by you, they both have somewhere else they need to be. For now, you remain completely calm as you know you will be leaving this hectic yet lifeless platform soon, once your train arrives. Use this moment as a time to pause. A momentary escape from the busy world, helping you see more clearly. The train you wait for, is taking you far away, where you will feel peace and calmness. You understand you will come back changed from this journey, for the better. You are excited and ready for it to begin.

Finally, your train pulls into the station and you step aboard. You decide that this time, this journey is devoted for yourself, to simply spend time with yourself, alone with no distractions. You take a seat and begin to relax completely, you understand this trip will allow you to gain a new perspective, which you know needs to be done. So allow yourself this time, and don't feel guilty. Now your sat, you place your heavy bag down, this fills you with a deep sense of relief. Your muscles are instantly soothed and relaxed. A sense of tranquility fills both your body and mind.

Now the train moves foward, the sound of the busy rush of people at the station begins to fade away and become replaced with a peaceful quiet. You look out the window as the train glides past the same grey world. This time you can observe it from a distance, and you feel less swallowed up by its miserable chaos. Although you are leaving behind this dull world now, you may feel sadness, regret or relief, either way you know now you are leaving behind all that held you back.

Use this time for rest and relaxation. Connect with your true self and your intentions, enabling you to see your needs and desires. Any sadness you feel or negative thoughts may be trying to tell you something. Perhaps these feelings are a result of neglecting the needs of your soul. In a way to grab your attention, you unintentionally create these unpleasant feelings. Either way, you using this time to care for yourself, and relax your entire body now.

Now the train has gained some distance from your current life, you can see your life from a whole new perspective. As you look out the window, the world outside seems different. The world seems to be filled with more colour, the sky a clear blue, the trees an emerald green, not dull at all.

As you move further away from the train station, a sense of easiness grows within you, you feel at peace. You are completely relaxed and calm. Your body sinks into the comfortable chair. You arms rested from the heavy baggage you carry. Your breathing slow and steady. Your legs and feet relaxed and light. Your mind has slowed to a steady pace, filled with clarity. You feel free, in perfect balance and happy how everything seems to be working out.

Now the train stops, it has reached your destination. You pick up your large, black, heavy bag, although now it feels seemingly lighter. You walk calmly off the train, you have just a few streets to walk down, before you reach your speacil awaiting place.

The bag still seems to weigh you down slightly, but you know you can hold out until you reach your destination. You feel stronger, more powerful and determined. It will all be over soon.

Now, you stand infront of a large metal gate. With some effort, you open it and let yourself in. You are in your very own private garden. It's been quite a while since you were here last. The place looks neglected. While you have been occupied by sadness and pain, there was no one to take care of it. But now, you are ready to take care of it once more. You step on the path, that winds gently through your garden. There are no longer any flowers and grass, instead grows thick weeds and brambles. You walk towards an old tree at the back of the garden. Leaning against the trees soft bark is a large spade. You pick it up and decide to dig a large hole, in the shade of the tree. Now you have finished digging, you decide to open up your large bag. Your are curious as to what heavy baggage you have been carrying around for so long, and to your surprise you find all your worries, doubts, fears and regrets. You see them as heavy, large, grey stones. You decide its time to let go, placing them into the huge hole you have just dug. As you drop each stone into the hole one by one, name these hard feelings and mentally say to each "I'm letting you go."

So now:

Let go of sadness.

Let go of anger.

Let go of doubt.

Let go of regrets.

Let go of the pain.

Let go of hopelessness.

Let go of resentment.

Let go of bitterness.

Let go of jealousy.

Let go of hate.

Let go of misery.

Let go of helplessness.

Let go of fear.

Let go of suffering.

Let go of uniformity.

Let go of all that makes you feel bad.

Repeat this, for as long as you need, letting go of all the stones from your bag, and finishing by burying the bag, too. Then cover the hole wil soil and feel the amazing relief.

Your eyes drift to an old bench that sits in the middle of the garden, you follow your gaze and take a seat on its warm, brown wood. As you sit here peacefully you feel at ease and completely free. Your body seems lighter, your muscles more loose. The sun above, shines down in beams through the tree's branches. Observe this garden and its current state, to fix it all and bring back its old glow, will only require a little of your energy. Giving this garden the care it deserves becomes a priority now, and you know you will enjoy the process as well as the results.

For now, just rest deeply on this bench, and imagine its final look after you have given it the care it needs. Inhale sunlight. Exhale tension. Imagine the delicate, colourful flowers. Smell the sweet roses. Feel your enthusiasm, your excitement to return the garden to a state of beauty. Realize the journey you took to get you here, was to remind you of who you really are. Smile, for your old self is back, who you really are. Simply enjoy the light as it dances around, avoiding the shadows in your garden, and mentally repeat to yourself:

I am free.

I am calm.

I am in peace.

I am grateful.

I am light.

I am happy.

I am full of love.

I am full of energy.

I am relaxed.

I am safe.

I am strong.

I am in control.

Life is good.

Life is colorful.

Life is amazing.

I love myself.

I know my worth and value.

I thankful for myself.

I accept myself.

I love life.

Now repeat these one more time:

I am free.

I am calm.

I am in peace.

I am grateful.

I am light.

I am happy.

I am full of love.

I am full of energy.

I am relaxed.

I am safe.

I am strong.

I am in control.

Life is good.

Life is colorful.

Life is amazing.

I love myself.

I know my worth and value.

I thankful for myself.

I accept myself.

I love life.

Inhale deeply and smile to yourself with your every exhale.

Just enjoy this relaxed state for a while, feeling the warm sunlight touch your skin, blessing you with its positive energy. You can take this feeling around with you as you move foward.

After you arrive home from this trip, and return to your everyday life, you will find you have been blessed with a completely new perspective.

Your private garden always waits for your return. So, don't feel a sadness as you leave, you can return whenever you wish and carry on the work with your garden.

So now, whenever your ready, gently open your eyes, returning to your day and its usual activities. Or, if you wish, keep your eyes closed and drift off into a deep, relaxing sleep.

Guided Meditation For Stress Relief

Welcome. This meditation guides you into providing you with the relief from stress you require. In today's busy world stress seems to be a common problem, that is so often looked past as normal. Generally, we don't even realize how stressed we are until we take a step back. Stress in some levels can actually be good for us, helping us stay alert and more productive, allowing us to reach certain goals and achievements. However, when stress becomes chronic, it becomes exhausting, draining all of our energy and negatively impacting all aspects of life. This is why intentionally setting aside time for stress relief and relaxation is so beneficial for you.

So feel free to use this meditation at times of particular stress, as well as the techniques we use here today. This may be before or after a stressful, tense event.

Now you are ready, find a quiet, comfortable place, where you know you won't be disturbed for the duration of this meditation. Turn off anything that could distract you, and consciously give this time solely to your well-being. You deserve this time, to simply relax and feel some relief. Naturally, are body and mind should feel at ease and relaxed. We are just taught from a young age to be stressed all the time. You body and mind need time to process our experiances, challenges, to rest, recharge and heal itself, which stress so often prevents. Now we are providing it with this time, to do all it needs.

Imagine I am here, sat with you, helping you lower your stress level, helping you feel more calm, and alleviated from the burden of stress you carry daily.

To provide you with the stress relief you need, we'll focus on three levels - your breath, your body, and your mind. The goal of which is to slow and deepen your breathing, relax your entire body and to completely calm the mind.

Understand it is okay to have thoughts that intrude your mind, this is expected during meditation, so not something you need to stress over. Allow yourself to simply remian in this moment of time. Let go of expectations and judgement you may have over this meditation, and simply enjoy all it brings to you. Just remain present here, and completely open.

Elongate your spine, allowing it to rest neutrally where is most natural. If you are sat, make sure your back is straight, yet not tensed. If your are in a lying position, make sure your spine is straight yet relaxed, as well. Either way make sure you take a comfortable, effortless position. Now prepare yourself for a deep sense of relaxation and close your eyes.

Shift your focus inward, and observe your breath. Notice its entire pathway through your body. Feel how the air effortlessly flows into your nostrils, down into your lungs and expands your stomach. Then, feel all the sensations it provides you as it leaves your stomach, then your lungs, and finally as it travels out through your nose. This process, so seemingly simple, is one of the most important connections between ourselves and life. So, notice even the tiniest of movements that connect with your breathing. In every moment there is always so much going on within our bodies, even if we may feel we are doing nothing. Notice all the sensations in the body that your breath provokes now, observing how they make you feel.

Now, let us work on deepening your breath further through the use of counting. So inhale, to the count of four. One, two, three, four.

Hold your breath as you do so, counting to three. One, two, three.

Exhale, to the count of six. One, two, three, four, five, six.

Now, repeat once more.

Inhale - one, two, three, four.

Hold - one, two, three.

Exhale - one, two, three, four, five, six.

Now, as you breathe in, visualize that you are collecting all the stress from all over your body, into a large pile. Breathe out slowly, as if you are gently blowing a dandelion. Allow this huge pile of stress, to be released with your breath.

Repeat this once again, and mentally round up all the stress and tension that remains in your body. Now, blow it all out.

Inhale, as you do so breathing in peace and tranquility. Allow these sensations to fill your stomach and lungs. Slowly exhale, mentally telling yourself: relax.

Once again, inhale deeply, taking in peace, and relaxation. Then, exhale slowly, repeating to yourself: relax.

Simply enjoy this moment, with your deep, relaxed, and slow breathing. Whenever thoughts appear, briefly notice them, before letting them pass by. Then, gently return your focus back to your breath and its pathway through your body and all the sensations this air provokes within you.

Using mindful awareness on the sensations of your body and focused attention on your breath, are effective practices for reducing stress rapidly, replacing it with feelings of relaxation. So feel free to use these techniques in everyday life, because as long as you live, your breath will always be with you, accompanying you through every challenge.

Stress in high levels has the power to interupt the body's running on so many levels. It can interfere with your blood flow, raising your blood pressure as well as your heart rhythm. It can use its influence to work on all the organs and cells of our body. Our mind also suffers, even our skin. Our brilliant bodies have the power and knowledge to heal themselves. However, when stress flows through us untamed, it becomes impossible. It's just like an organ slowly releasing poison, that we know how to heal from, but we can't compete with its continuous flow. This is why practising this meditation regularly and learning how to release stress is so tremendously beneficial.

Now, we will work on relaxing the body part by part. When your body is completely relaxed, your mind often follows, so it is important to relax the entire body. We will do this by tensing each part of the body, before allowing it to sink into complete relaxation.

So, let's start with the very bottom of your body, before working towards the very tip of our heads. Turn your awareness to your toes. Take a deep breath in and tense up the whole feet. Hold this breath and the tensed muscles in your feet and count to three. One, two, three. Now release your breath and your feet, relaxed.

With your next inhale, tense up your lower legs and knees. Hold it all there – one, two, three. And relax.

Now, take another deep breath in, this time tensing and contracting your upper legs, glutes and hips as tightly as you can. Hold- one, two, three. And release this tightness as you exhale.

Inhale, clenching your fists. Hold everything there, till three. One, two, three. Exhale slowly, releasing your grip, and allowing your fingers to spread naturally wheres comfortable. Relax your palms, letting them open up against the ceiling. Relax your wrists.

Take a deep breath in and tighten your lower arms, elbows and upper arms. Hold your breath for the next moment. One, two, three. Release all. Feel as all the muscles in your arms loosen, becoming lighter and more free.

Inhale, tensing and compressing your shoulders into your ears. Hold everything here. One, two, three, and release your breath and any tension here. Your shoulders seem less heavy and weighed down by your arms now.

With your next breath in, remain with your shoulders. Here, within our bodies we so often hold the burden of all our stress, worries and tension. So place your attention here as you hold your breath. One, two, three. Breathe out and let all the weight drop from your shoulders, completely relaxed.

Now inhale, contracting your abdominal muscles as tightly as you can as this air flows in. Pull these muscles to your spine, feeling the tension. Hold for a moment—one, two, three, and release. Let your stomach relax and allow its movements to return in synch with your breaths rhythm.

With your next breath, fill your lungs, expanding and tensing your chest. Hold as I count: one, two, three. Breathe out, releasing and relaxing your chest. Notice your ribcage now, as if its floating free, completely relaxed.

Next, move to the muscles of your back. Inhale, stretching it so it stands taller and notice all the tension in your back and spine. Hold your breath- one, two, three. Exhale, relaxing all the back muscles, one by one, so your spine is sat neutrally, straight and comfortable.

Repeat this for the neck now.

Inhale, tensing and stretching the muscles of your neck. Hold –one, two, three. Breathe out, and relax your neck. Your head seems even lighter now, your neck supporting it with ease.

With the next breath, notice the tension you feel in your scalp. Stay with these sensations for one, two, three. Breathe out and release, allowing your scalp to relax.

Now moving to your forehead, notice the intense tension in your forehead. This part often remains tense from overthinking, and never has the opportunity to relax. So breathe in, tensing it even more by raising your eyebrows. Remain here, holding this tension for- one, two, three. Then release. Now this tension finally drifts away, leaving you relaxed and calm.

Inhale, squeezing your eyes, and all the tiny eye muscles that surround them. Hold everything tight for one, two, three. Then, exhale and release all tension, allowing your eyes to relax. Now these muscles are alleviated from this tension, let your eyes sink gently into your head.

With your next breath, clench your teeth and jaw tightly together. Hold it to three. One, two, three. Breathe out and release. Allow your jaw to rest in its natural position, dropped down so your teeth don't touch. Let your tongue rest softly between, with your lips resting gently over your teeth. Your whole mouth completely releaxed.

Now we have worked through tensing and then relaxing your whole body completely. Scan through your body once more, noticing any tension that remains, clinging onto you. As you come across any tension, consciously and intentionally place relaxation there, breathing into the area and relaxing it completely.

If any stress still gathers in any corner or shadow of your body, allow it to collect on the surface. From here, the power of your breath alone can transport it away, out with your exhale.

A tense body is the result of a stressed mind. Since your body is now completely relaxed, it sends powerful signals to your mind alerting it that everything is fine, you are safe, that it can relax too. Allowing stress to drift away.

Now, your breathing is steady, deep and slow, and your body in a state of calm and relaxation, it is time for your mind to slow and become relaxed as well.

Our minds are the creator of most of our stress. It is normal to for it to produce numerous thoughts which we follow into a tangent. This means our minds become overwhelmed by the ever increasing burden of worry, fears, to-do lists and scenarios of what might or could of been. Our minds become a place of constant chaos and rush, and need the time to slow down and relax. Many health issues and conditions source, is the mind itself. So it is crucial that we learn how to soothe our minds from there heavy burdens, giving them the time to rest and recharge. Even something so powerful and wise, your brain, requires rest from time to time.

Once you accept the fact that there will always be thoughts passing through your mind, you will be able to relax on a deeper level. It is normal for these thoughts to flow by, as their production is part of the mind's role. So, don't let their presence stress you out at all.

Now, take a deep breath in. Notice the first thought that arises in your mind. Rather than engaging with it, just observe it. Then, as you breathe out, let it go.

Repeat this, with your next thought, noticing as the thought begins to form in your mind. Take a deep breath in, holding as this thought arises. Exhale, and release.

Notice how the thoughts passing through are beginning to slow, as they line up with the steady rhthym of your breath.

Although the frequency of thoughts seems to have slowed, some thoughts appear very fast, like a bouncing ball. As these appear, catch it, thowing them as far away as you can. Other thoughts arise just like big beach balls, more slowly. Some thoughts appear even slower, gently drifting over, like a balloon. Catch them briefly, and without too much force that would pop them, let them float by. As time goes on and your thoughts pass in synchrony with your breath, there will be less bouncing balls, and more slower and lighter balloons that gently float by. This means you have more control over their stay in your mind, as you should be able to gently tap them away.

You can also use this moment to imagine any harder, more heavily impacting thoughts, that result in stress, as a dark cloud. Imagine you lay under the sky. Each small dark, cloud in the sky represents a hard thought. These clouds range in colour from a light grey, to a deep black, depending on how stressful the thought behind it is.

Once every last even slightly stressful or worrying thought has been placed into the sky, you are ready to feel relief. Focus your attention onto one of these dark clouds and the stressful thought that you created it for. Inhale, and as you exhale imagine you are releasing stress. As you do this, watch this cloud as it changes colour, becoming lighter and lighter, untill its an inviting white and fluffy cloud.

Move to the next cloud now. Breathe in, and collect all your stress and darkness from the cloud. Breathe out, let go, and watch as the cloud becomes a snow white.

Inhale, moving to the next cloud, taking up all the darkness from the cloud and its thought. Exhale, breathing it all out.

Continue to do this for a while, focusing on each and every cloud until they all become a pearly white. Allow yourself to feel at ease, enjoying the escape away from your stressful thoughts. Now, they don't seem hard or dark anymore, and you feel your burden has become lighter and more easy.

Now, take a deep breath in. Exhale, and as you do so, imagine you are blowing the first white cloud away. It drifts away and slowly disappears in the distance. Where the cloud once was, is now a clear blue sky. Breathe in, repeating this process with the next cloud. Breathe out, blowing it away, leaving behind an even clearer sky.

Inhale and whilst you exhale repeat for all the rest of the clouds in your sky. Blowing them all away.

Above you is a clear, blue sky, free from any clouds. Your mind, like the sky is clear from any stressful thought. Enjoy this liberating sense of calmness, easiness, and lightness, as it spreads over you. Your mind is completely relaxed now.

Now your mind is completely calm and relaxed, return your focus to your breath.

With each breath you take, mentally repeat these affirmations to yourself:

Inhale, exhale. I am calm.

Breathe in through your nose. I am relaxed. Breathe out through your mouth.

Breathe deeply in. I feel light and at ease. Breathe out slowly.

I feel at peace.

I am confident.

I am strong.

I am focused.

Inhale and say to yourself: I can handle anything that life throws my way. Breathe out.

There is love within me.

Breathe in through your nose. I feel relaxed. Breathe out through your mouth.

I am intelligent.

I am powerful.

I am amazing.

I feel enthusiasm towards life.

Inhale. I make peace with everything inside and outside me. Exhale gently.

I enjoy the sensation as all my cells are filled with relaxation.

I bring light with me wherever I go.

I am in control and can handle everything with ease.

Breathe in through your nose. I am in perfect harmony. Breathe out.

I am calm. Breathe out.

Breathe in through your nose. I feel rejuvenated. Breathe out through your mouth.

I feel refreshed.

I feel re-energized.

I am skillful.

I am focused.

Inhale. I can handle anything that life brings me. Exhale.

I am filled with peace.

I am filled with joy.

Breathe in. Continuing to repeat these affimations to yourself.

I am relaxed. Breathe out.

I am intelligent.

I am powerful.

I am amazing.

I feel enthusiasm towards life.

Inhale. I make peace with everything outside and outside me. Exhale gently.

I enjoy the sensation as all my cells are filled with relaxation.

I bring light with me, wherever I go.

I am in control and can handle everything with ease.

Breathe in through your nose. I am in harmony. Breathe out.

Notice your body now, feeling it relaxed from head to toe. Feel the surface beneath you, completely supporting you. As you sit or lay here, imagine a cloud slowly forming underneath you. Now this cloud has grown to the size of your body, and it is the softest most comfortable thing you have ever rested on. It's supporting you perfectly, cradling and protecting your relaxed body from stress and worry, completely soft yet secure. So enjoy this moment, and simply rest on this cloud. It's here for only you.

The cloud slowly begins to drift upwards, elevating you further and further from the ground. As you float higher into the sky, you don't feel scared at all, you know you are safe here with this cloud. So enjoy this restful experiance.

Below you is the land. From high up in the sky, everything seems so small from here, and you feel comforted by how small you would look from below. You see green fields, winding rivers, old pointy mountains, you see so much. The landscape looks just like a loved, warm and colourful quilt. Now, you take a look for all those things that used to provoke your stress, from here you cant even see them! Yet these things held so much power over you. Here, on your fluffy cloud, all your troubles, worries, financial and health problems, can't bother and stress you, as they are left far down on the ground. Here, all you feel is just relaxation, peace and a feeling of ease.

Suddenly, a golden light begins to shine from the centre if your cloud. It looks just like a small sun, is shining from right behind it. The light grows stronger and stronger, so much so that the whole cloud is illuminated by this light. This light continues to grow, now moving onto your body, spreading from the points at which you touch the cloud. Your feet are now glowing, your whole legs shining. You feel as this light spreads up through to your stomach and chest, now golden. This golden light penetrates through into your arms and hands, they glow brightly too. Now your head is radiating the light too. Your whole body illuminated with this golden light. You can visably see this golden light shining from you, but you can also feel as it gently enwraps your organs and cells inside you. It fills your heart, so it now pumps this golden light around your body, just as it does blood. This light holds a healing, relaxing power, relieving you of stress. As it spreads through you, you become consumed by peace and calmness. It is everywhere, in your every cell, even your every thought. Now there is now darkness for stress to hide, so all the stress you once carried feels like a distant memory. You don't ever have to carry around so much stress, as this cloud and its golden light is never far away. For now, just bathe in this refreshing golden light, enjoying this present moment.

Now your body and mind are completely relaxed. You have drained all your stress away, and you feel liberated and free. Your breathing is deep, slow and steady, your mind filled with clarity, and your body completely relaxed. Your cloud drifts back down to the ground now. So whenever you're ready, slowly get up and depart from your cloud, ready and re-energiized.

Gently open your eyes, and return to your day, feeling completely renewed and stress-free.

Guided Meditation for Sleep- The Magic Garden (30 Minutes)

Hello and welcome to this sleep meditation. I will guide you through a journey, where you will reach deep sleep. So before we begin, get nice and comfortable in your bed. Make sure you are the perfect temperature for sleep, so not too hot or cold, as this will only occupy your busy mind later on.

To begin your journey, into a restful nights sleep we will begin by releaxing your body. When your body is completely relaxed, it sends signals to your mind telling it it is free to relax also.

So, imagine you find yourself sat or lying down on a large bench in the corner of a beautiful garden. The sun above, is starting to rise over the edges of the warm stone walls of the garden. The sun's golden light now casts your feet into brightness. This light feels soothingly warm. Inhale, allowing this powerful light to sink deep into your feet. Exhale, breathing out any tension your held there. Your feet feel calm and relaxed.

Slowly, this light spreads up, reaching your knees. You inhale deeply, allowing this light to spread deep into your lower legs, pushing away all your stresses, worries and fears away, ready to be exhaled. Now, this light has moved further into the garden, illuminating your upper legs and hips. Again, you breathe in allowing this light to completely enter. Enjoy the sensation as it spreads through you, filling your legs with its relaxing energy. Breathe out, allowing your breath to carry away any tension the light displaced.

The warm light of day continues to slowy move over your whole body, sending each part into deep relaxation. Continue to inhale, allowing this light to completely enter you, before exhaling any tension from your body. Just enjoy the sensations your body feels as it sinks deeper into relaxation. Now the light not only illuminates your body, part by part, but also the edges of the garden, hitting the plants. Like you, the plants seem to feel the powerful energy of this light, stretching and standing up taller, ready for this new day. The sun continues to rise, higher in the sky, hitting the small bushes and bouncing of the surface of the small pond in the centre of the garden.

Tonight, we will continue to explore this magical garden, allowing its enchanting powers to wash over you, relaxing you further and further, until you are ready to greet a nights restful sleep.

The sun has now moved high into the sky, so the whole garden is no longer in shadow, but in full sunlight. Your entire body is cast in this golden light. Take another deep breath, feeling as this light spreads through you, past your skin and into your every organ and system. Notice it on your forehead now, feeling its warmth, soothing your muscles, enabling you to release all tension here, so it rests completely relaxed. Infact, every last muscle in your body has been touched by this soft light, becoming more loose and light, entirely relaxed.

You look around the garden now, it seems to be wonderfully cared for, the fish in the pond healthly fed, the grass cut perfectly, no flower out of place and not a single weed in sight. The gardens beauty amazes you, for such a large space to be this perfect, it must be a miracle! You imagine you could take a pleasant stroll in this garden not matter the weather, simply because it is so wonderful.

As you sit, comfortably on the bench, notice everything there is to sense here. Listen to the sounds of the gentle breeze as it rustles through the grass and trees, notice the chirp of the crickets in the grass, and the soft song of the birds in their nests. There is so many animals that are lucky enough to call this garden home. Now, smell the potent scent of the roses as they have risen for the day. Look around at the colourful flowers, they're placment perfectly selected in rows of different colours. Just enhoy this moment, right here, in this pleasant garden.

As we move foward, through this journey of relaxation, you may find your mind wanders, bringing random thoughts and worries. If so, don't be alarmed, this is normal behaviour. Throughout your day, your mind is in constant use and may not be used to having the time to switch of and slow down. As you begin to give your mind this time to rest, it reacts by producing thoughts, with time and practise you can begin to switch of more, giving yourself the much needed time to rest, allowing you to reach a deeper, more relaxing sleep.

So, when random thoughts do arise, acknowledge their prescence briefly, rather than ignoring their existance. Then allow them to pass, bringing your focus to your breath, to this present moment, to this beautiful garden. So do this as your next thought arises. Feel the thought forming, then briefly notice it. Shift your focus back to your breath, helping to ground you in this present moment. Inhale, and exhale, allowing this thought to pass, just like the air from your body. Repeat this process with every thought, enabling you to remain in the here and now, and not distracting by any thoughts, worries or concerns.

Look around the garden once more. Part of the magic of this garden is its maintanance, there seems to be no gardener, yet it remains a utopian. This garden is open for all, yet it is so early in the day you are here alone. There is some small tasks here you decide will improve others experiance in the day. On the cobbled path, some leaves lay, blown over by the nights wind. To one side of your bench, lays a broom. You pick up the broom, walk over to the path ready to sweep the colourful leaves away. As you get nearer you notice these leaves are dark, black and crispy. Old and unwanted leaves no longer effective, just like your worries, stresses and fears, not serving your true intentions. Imagine these leaves as your darker, harder thoughts and emotions.

You begin to sweep these leaves away, beginning to clear both the path and your mind. To begin, you focus on the larger, darker and older leaves, the ones that seem to have been here a while. These leaves, are thoughts, fears, anger, guilt which you have been holding onto for too long, weighing you down. With focus and control, you sweep these leaves far away into the distance, clearing the path. Move onto the next big, dark leaf now. Again, with intention and focus you sweep this leaf away, off the path and no longer carried by you. You begin to feel lighter and your mind more clear. You continue to use your undivided focus to sweep this path clear, until no leaves remain. Your mind now liberated from these thoughts and emotions, you feel a sense of calm and peace wash over you. Remain with these sensations in your body for a moment, enjoying the sense of relaxation within you.

Now, the pathway is clear you walk over to the fountain, by the centre of the garden. The light glistens of the wild bubbly yet relaxing water, and you notice by the edge is a small net. You know what you need to do, you pick up the net, and begin to fish out the leaves from the fountain. Luckily there is not to many old leaves in the fountain, so you get to work. As you begin to clear the leaves, you look at the shiny, golden coins that rest at the bottom. There seems to be lots in the bottom, so you wonder if right now, there is something in the air, that makes peoples wishes come true. You pause for a moment, thinking about anything you would wish for. Maybe for confidence as you face a new challenge? Control over your emotions? Remaining stress free and relaxed? Whatever it may be, you think of it, as you toss a large gold coin into the fountain, that rested in your pocket all along.

Now, you return to your task of clearing the leaves from the fountain. Again each of these old leaves, represent any unpleasant thoughts. You focus on sifting these smaller leaves out of the fountain. Finally the fountain's waters seem crystal clear, not a single peice of debris float about. Like the fountain your mind is filled with clearness and clarity, no longer suffering from these thoughts you can focus on the present completely. As your mind is now, enirely relaxed.

Right now, you watch the beautiful fountain for a moment, simply taking in the majesty of the falling water. Simply enjoy the wonders of this garden completely, remaining right here, in the now. If thoughts to arise, return your focus to your breath. Feel every sensation this new refreshing air you inhale provokes. Notice how the air flows through your nose, expanding your lungs, and back out through your mouth again. Stay grounded in the present aware of the sensations of your body, feeling as you sink further into relaxation.

You turn your attention to the pond now, observing as the fish effortlessly glide through the water. As you peer over the edge of the water, the fish notice your prescence rising up to the surface, hoping you will provide them with their morning food. Searching around you notice a small tub of fish food to the right of the pond, you grab a small handful, scattering it over the water's surface. As you do so, the fish rush up to the surface in excitement, ready for their breakfast. You watch as they hoover up the food quickly, as if they've never been fed. You feel tempted to give them more, although you know you shouldn't over feed them. Instead, you turn your back on them, returning your attention to the rest of the garden.

You walk around the garden, enjoying the feeling of stillness. At this time of morning, even though no one else is around, you can still sense the activity in the garden. The feeling in the air is soothing, you are alone, but don't feel it all. The sense of flowers and trees reacting to the arrival of day fills you, filling you with their positive yet relaxing energy.

The soothing, warm energy in the garden, and the small tasks you've completed seem to have tired you. You head towards the large oak tree at the back of the garden. It is the largest oldest tree in the garden and under the shelter of its leaves seems like a pleasant place to sit and rest. You sit, leaning against its trunk, admiring its impressive size and beauty. From here you can also look out onto the whole garden, appriciating its calm, enchating allure. You feel completely relaxed and calm. This garden must truely be magic!

You sit enjoying the feelings of tranquility, peace, and harmony that fill you. Continuing to observe all this garden has to offer, and all that are lucky enough to call this garden home. Wondering about what over wishes will be made into this garden's fountain, you drift of into a restful, refreshing sleep.

Guided Meditation Returning To Sleep (30 Minutes)

Welcome to this guided meditation which will help you drift back into sleep. Waking up in the middle of the night can be very frustrating, especially if you feel wide awake and returing to sleep seems impossible. Often, this frustration is actually what prevents us sleeping once again. So, allowing yourself to slowly power down, without getting too frustrated, is important. Only once this has occured, you can return to sleep, so you can feel refreshed and ready to go in the morning.

So to begin, make sure you are ready for sleep. Lie down in bed, making yourself comfortable. Ensure you are the perfect temperature for sleep, so if your cold nestle yourself under the sheets, or remove a layer if too hot. It's important that you are able to relax both your mind and body, so maintaining the body in comfort is important as this will only distract you from sleep. Even if you are not able to drift back into sleep, just by following this meditation and relaxing the body and mind, will help you feel refreshed and energized in the morning.

So take a deep breath in, from your stomach. Then, slowly breathe out. As the air leaves your body, allow it to bring you relaxation. Take another deep breath in, exhale slowly and gently releasing any tension and frustration outside you. Now return your breathing to its natural rhythm. Allow yourself to breathe peacefully.

As you place your focus with your breath, notice how much more relaxed you have become alreday. Right now, there is nothing else you need to focus on, nothing else needs to occupy your mind. Just focus on the ins and outs of your breath. Placing your attention here, you will become more and more tired and sleepy.

Now with your next exhale, see how slowly you can release the air. Take a big, deep breath in and then slowly exhale. Very slowly and gently, see how slow you can release this breath from you. As you do this, your body can truly recognise and appriciate the relaxing sensations of your breath. Repeat this again, seeing how slowly you can exhale, before allowing your breath to return to its usual pattern.

Allow the pathway of the air you breathe, to flow through you, as it usually would. Breathe in and out without any effort and extra thought. Just trusting in your body's natural pace. Calm, soft and comfortable.

Now place your complete attention with your body. Allow your body to feel completely relaxed. Notice the stillness of your leg muscles, how heavy and warm they are. Feel how this warmth in your legs, begins to spread through your entire body. Slowly you become more and more comfortable, sinking deeper into relaxation.

Notice your shoulders as they begin to relax. Allow them to loosen and release the tension you hold there. They relax, dropping down, liberated from the weight you usually carry. Observe as your arms get heavier. This feeling of heaviness takes over your whole body and you sink deeper and deeper into your bed. Totally relaxed and comfortable.

Feel the warmth in your hands now. Appreciate this soothing sensation as this warmth spreads up into your arms, taking over your shoulders.

If your eyes are still open, notice now how they feel. Blink, observing how heavy your eyelids feel. If you desire, close your eyes, allowing your eyelids to gently rest over your eyes. Feel as your eyes sink into their sockets, completely relaxed. Now move your awareness to your forehead, notice the cool air that touches it. How smooth and relaxed it feels, free from tension.

With each exhale, imagine any feelings of tension gently flow out of you. Simply draining away, so you become more and more relaxed. Without your resistance allow this tension to drain out of you. You no longer need it.

If your mind slowly starts to drift away, don't be alarmed. Don't force anything. Just allow your mind to drift away, as if its moving down a calm beautiful river. Your focus doesn't need to remain with anything, there is nothing that needs to occupy your mind. Just embrace the feelings of calm and relaxation, allowing the feelings of tiredness enter.

As you allow your mind to move as it wishes, you will notice the tension within drift away, and become replaced with feelings of relaxation. Enjoy the feeling of soft, warmth spread through you, as you sink deeper into your bed. Let calmness and peace in. You are completely balanced and in harmony. Devoting his time for only you, and your relaxation, to rest and recharge.

Now, shift your focus back to your breath. Begin to count each and every breath. Inhaling, one. Exhaling, one. Inhaling, two. Exhaling, two. Continue to count, untill you reach five and then begin at one again. Notice as you count, you move further towards a peaceful sleep.

Continue to count your breaths. Focus on each number and the breath, in and out. If you find yourself losing count, as your mind wanders, that's okay. Just return to one and start again. Just continue counting, feeling more and more relaxed. With every number that passes, you feel more heavy, more relaxed. It becomes harder and harder to maintain your focus on the counting. You move closer to a restful, refreshing sleep.

Your mind begins to wander more, drifting further away. Drifting closer and closer to sleep. If your able to, return your mind back to the counting of your breath. Inhale, one. Exhale, one. In for two. Out for two. A sense of sleepiness washes over you, and it becomes even harder to count. For as long as possible, return your mind back to the counting.

Your body feels lighter, almost weightless like a feather. You seem to be floating in a cool breeze, yet sinking deeper into the comfort of your bed. Continue to return your mind to the counting. Inhale, one. Exhale, one. In for two. Out for two. Inhale, three. Exhale, three.

With each passing number, the sense of peace, calmness and relaxation spreads through your body further. Your body and mind, seem to greet each other in a sea of relaxation. Slowly drifting into sleep. You have no lingering frustration about your sleep being disturbed, no more thoughts to keep you awake. So, just calmly drift off, at your own pace.

Inhale, one. Exhale, one. Inhale two. Exhale, two. Inhale, three. Exhale, three.

Allow yourself to fully experience the sensation of relaxing sleep now. Your mind and body are totally free from tension and intrusive thoughts. A sense of calm has sunk deep into you as you drift off, back to sleep. You will wake in the morning, feeling completely refreshed, re-energized and ready to tackle anything your day throws at you.

Guided Meditation for sleep- The Birds Of The Mountain Forest (30 Minutes)

Hello and welcome to this journey through the mountain forest, to sleep. In this meditation we will travel through the forest, taking in all the sights and sounds, moving towards a deep state of relaxation, allowing you to drift into a deep, peaceful sleep.

So before we begin this journey, make sure you are comfortable. Lie down in your bed, get cozy under the covers so you are a perfect temperature. Discomfort will only distract you later on, so make sure you are nestled into your bed, completely comfortable. Take a deep breath in and then slowly exhale. As you breathe out, allow any tension in your body to be released. So if you are ready, let our journey begin.

Surprisingly, many peple who visit forests in the mountains often say they don't come across many signs of life. Of course all sorts of vegetation surrounds them, although they get the impression that nothing else has lived in these forests for years. Chances are though, the animals that live there have merely been scared away by the strangers presence. To connect with all aspects of nature in the mountain forests, you have to release all tension and negative thoughts, in order for the animals to trust you. By releasing all this negative energy from within you, you can truely connect to your surroundings absorbing its positive, relaxing energy.

So to begin, turn your attention to your breathing. Take a deep breath in, feeling as the cool, refreshing air moves from your nose, into your lungs and around your body. Exhale, breathing out hot tense air. Enjoy the sensations this enchanting forest air provokes in your body, filling you with a sense of relaxation. Repeat again, inhaling slowly and deeply, filling your lungs with this magical air. Now, exhale slowly releasing any stressful, negative thoughts and emotions as you do so. Allow your breath to return to its natural rhythm, continuing to be soothed by this fresh mountain air.

Now, shift your focus to where you find yourself, in the mountain forest. Fully take in all your surroundings, the vast variety of trees, with their impressive range of sizes and shaped leaves. Some of these trees that tower over you have been here for hundreds of years. They stand tall on the mountain side provding a safe haven for a number of insects, birds and squirels. The only thing that stands any taller is the mountains themselves, that poke out of the sea of green trees.

Notice the calm feeling the forest generates, allow it to penetrate deep inside of you, into your every cell, relaxing you. As you are filled with this calming energy and you begin to become more and more relaxed, the shy animals of the forest will begin to reveal themselves to you.

You would love to see the life that calls this forest home, so let us begin to relax you body completely. You make your way towards a large oak tree and sit against its trunk. Now, we will slowly scan through your entire body, looking for any signs of tension. So to begin place your entire focus with the very top of your head and forehead. Take a deep breath in, and then exhale slowly releasing any tension here. Notice now your muscles here seem looser and more relaxed. Moving down, place your attention with every last tiny muscle in your face. Breath in, and out releasing any tension here, relaxing your face completely. If you haven't done so already, let your eyelids rest softly over your eyes, and let them sink further into your head. Continue to move down your body for the next few momoments, scanning for any signs of tension. Allow your breath to carry away, any worries and stresses that reside in your body.

(Pause for 1 minute.)

Now as you move towards the very tips of your toes, most, if not all of the tension within you has been carried away by the air you breath. Enjoy this feeling, liberated from those negative thoughts you carry around, that prevent you from reaching relaxation and fulfilling sleep.

More and more relaxed, you return you gaze to your surroundings. Above you a red squirell, stands on a branch looking down at you. It can sense you are more calm and trusts your presence, revealing itself as it stands gazing at a large nut. It takes a moment to gauge the size of this nut, wondering if it will provide him the right amount of fuel for the day, or if it will have to go foraging for more later. It briefly stares down at you, with large inviting eyes, welcoming you to the forest, before moving swiftly onwards with his prized nut.

You appreciate the trust the squirell placed with you, and it feels you with a warm calmness. Enjoy the feelings the forest provides you with now, simply remaining in this present moment. You may find your mind brings about random negative thoughts that often consume you. This is a normal reaction, for a mind not used to rest and usually in constant use, so don't be alarmed. When these thoughts arise, briefly acknowledge them before allowing them to pass, then shift your focus back to your breath, grounding you to the present moment, to the mountain forest. Practise this process, with the next thought that arises, remaining here and calm.

For now, truely experiance all this forest has to offer. As you slip deeper into relaxation, you come across more signs of life. place your undivided focus attention here, and listen to the sounds of the forest. When you first arrived, the forest was a peaceful almost silence, now you can hear the soft murmers of life. In the distance you can hear the soothing sounds of a bird's song, the rustling of squirells in the branches above and the gentle buzz of insects in the sky. These sounds send you into a deep sense of peace and relaxation.

Your mind begins to slow now, and negative thoughts that consume you so often, seem like a distant memory. Give yourself this time, and allow yourself to be soothed by the forest. You look up now and see a small blue tit attempting to strip the bark from the tree. These small birds are quite swift and are easily startled, so it here in you prescence provides you with a sense of peace. You are grateful for its company here, and the trust it places in you, as it can sense your positive thoughts and energy, that you continue to absorb from the forest.

As your mind begins to slow, and you become more and more relaxed, the forest seems to awaken more. Overhead, you notice something fly swiftly past. It seems to have gone in a flash, but you recognized it as a bald eagle. You will probably see it once again before you are ready to leave, as they tend to circle these forests, looking for food. Most of the inhabitants of the forest live among the trees, but these bald eagles are different. They make their homes high up in the mountains, so every morning they look down at their domain, in complete control of their lives.

You get up and start to move around the forest, you start to consider the size of the trees in this forest, there is no wonder why there is such an abundance of life here. You are amazed you didn't recognize all of the life here at first, and were so distracted by your negative thoughts. You stand staring at the abandunce of trees around you, that provide a home for all sorts of species of colourful, majestic birds.

The sound of bird song grows louder now, filling you with a sense of harmony and soothing your mind from its usual streem of negative thoughts. As you relax further, this song seems to sink into your every last cell, filling you with a positive energy that moves you further into relaxation. Now, you are relaxed completely, and relieved from your thoughts. You feel at peace and ready to drift of into sleep.

So, make your way towards the edge of the forest, and as you move, more and more animals seem to trust you with their presence. Their company fills you with even more peace and calmness and you are so tired you can barely move fowards. At the edge of the forest further from the taller, older trees protection, limited vegatation grows. Despite this, you see a large number of all different types of birds. They gather on the nearby braches singing a beautiful song, as if they are saying goodbye to their visitor. The wonderful chorus is so relaxing, as you drift further and further away from the forest, you can still hear it in the distance, soothing you into a peaceful, rejuvenating night's sleep. This tranquil place always awaits your return, but for now goodbye, and maybe the animals will see you again soon. Goodnight.

Guided Meditation For Sleep & Anxiety Relief (40 Minutes)

Welcome to this guided sleep meditation. One of the aims of this meditation, is to gain relief from any stress and anxiety, you suffer from daily, weighing you down. Through the use of visualisation, we will transform these negative feelings into positive feelings, so you can begin to find peace and drift off into a deep, rejuvenating night's sleep.

So to prepare yourself for this moment, for peace. Take a moment to make sure you are completely comfortable. So, lay down in your bed, get yourself into a comfortable position, the covers on or off, so you are the perfect temperature.

Now, remain in the present, becoming aware of all the sensations in your body right now. Notice the soft surface of your bed beneath you, how comfortable it feels. How you are finally settled inside its warmth, after a long, restless day. Move your attention to your mind. How does it feel right now? Is it filled with anxious thoughts that seek your attention? These thoughts may already be on your mind, but that is okay. Struggling with anxious thoughts is a normal problem, and through this meditation you will eradicate them. By relieving you of these thoughts your body and mind can have a peaceful and productive night's sleep. Remember your are worthy of just that, so let's move foward with this meditation.

So, move you focus to the sound of my voice. Those intrusive thoughts may still be trying to fight for your attention, but simply allow these thoughts to slowly drift away, and they will begin to realise that there is no space for them right now. For now, all you need to focus on is my voice. So, if you haven't done so already, feel free to close your eyes. Notice how good that feels. The warm, soothing sensation as your eyelids rest closed over your eyes, and how it slowly spreads to your forehead and up to your scalp. Although this may feel great, you can keep your eyes open for now, until they feel ready and can't resist staying open any longer.

You may find you drift off to sleep before the end of the meditation. This is okay, you will still feel the benefits of the session as your unconscious still listens to what I'm saying, impacting you even if you drift away sooner.

Remain here, in this moment, it is for you alone. Embrace all you feel, and you will begin to notice time starts to slow. Each passing moment in the present, helps you feel more and more relaxed and positive, aiding you, as you deal with those feelings of anxiety.

Now, shift your awareness to your breath. Notice how your chest gently rises and falls with every inhale and exhale. Random thoughts and feelings may continue to arise in you, if so, let them pass by before returning your attention to your breathing. Notice the natural pattern of your breath, its depth, its frequency, how it begins to slow as you become filled with feelings of peace, relaxation and calmness.

Your breathing is a constant in your life. It keeps going no matter what your conscious mind is focused on. So if ever you become distracted by negative, hard thoughts use it to ground you to the present moment. Fully experiance your breath now, with your full concentration. This may feel strange if you have never done this before. These sensations you feel right now, are occuring within you in the present moment, and you aren't distracted by thoughts on the past of future, but with right now. As you focus completely on your breath now, enjoy the feelings of peace your mind recieves and deserves.

With every exhale you become more relaxed, moving into a complete state of peace. Notice the changes that have occured within you already. You feel more comfortable, tension seems to be slipping away, soothed by your breath. You are amazed that simply by focusing on your breathing, you have been able to slip into a wonderful, tranquil place of peace.

Now, take longer breaths. Inhale slowly and gently, and exhale for much longer than you usually would. As you breath in this rhythm, notice how your body seems to slip further into relaxation. Observe the rise and fall of your chest, how your stomach moves in connection with your breath too. Take a deep breath in, feeling as your chest and stomach rise. Then, breathe out, noticing as the muscles in your chest gradually relax and lower again. Enjoy this process, and the sensations the air provokes within you.

Allow your breath to return to its regular pattern. Experiance what it is like to have full control over your breath, as you begin to expand your awareness. Become aware of all your body feels, right from the very top of your head to the tips of your toes. As you do so, notice any tension you feel and where it resides within you. Take the next few moments to just notice any tension, and how it makes you feel.

Using the power of your imagination, visualize a large selection of candles in front of you. Each one represents a piece of tension within you. They flicker softly, attempting to grab you attention. So, take a quick moment to observe these candles prescence.

Now place your attention with one of the large candles as well as the tension it represents. Using your undivided attention here, take a deep breath in. Hold this breath inside you, allowing this refreshing air to move towards this tension. Exhale, allowing this tension to slowly drift away, blowing out that candle. The tension in that area seems to have slowly drained away, leaving you feeling relief. Now, turn to another candle. Place your focus with it and the tension it represents, and inhale. Then exhale, noticing this candle is now blown out.

As you continue to work on each candle, you release the stresses and tensions that were fueling your anxiety. By doing so, you provide your body and mind the space it requires to rest and recharge. As you cleanse your mind from these negative thoughts, you give it more space to be filled with positive thoughts and emotions. So allow yourself this time to rest and recharge, allowing you to enter sleep liberated from your pattern of negative thinking and stresses.

Move foward, continuing to blow out the candles one by one. Notice how you feel as you blow out each one, as you move closer to a peaceful night's sleep. You are so close to releasing all tension from your body, replacing it with positive energy.

Now, as you have less and less candles to blow out, notice how your body and mind communicate. Notice every signal between them, how these connections are beginning to blur. Now your body and mind, and the line between each is unclear, seemingly becoming one. They feel as if they are one entity, where you can truely sense all the different sensations relaxation brings. This feeling only greatens with each candle you blow out. Now your mind feels free, there is nothing stopping you fully experiancing the sense of calmness you feel. Another candle blown out, a stop towards complete balance, a step towards perfect rest.

Now just one candle remains lit. With one long exhalation blow it out. You feel completely liberated from stress, tension and anxiety. Now if you have room, stretch yourself out a little, making yourself as long as possible. Place your awareness with your breath, noticing how much it has slowed now. With every breath, you are becoming more relaxed.

Now you feel relaxed and peaceful, your mind may wander bringing up what gave you stress and anxiety today. Just observe these thoughts, these feelings are completely valid and aren't something you have to completely push away. Don't let these thoughts eat into your conscious mind, but let them briefly pass. If these thoughts becoming too distracting, and you begin to engage in them, bring your mind back to your breathing, to the present moment, where you are completely relaxed.

Any anxious feelings, stressed emotions and recurring negative thoughts that remain, imagine them as balloons. Let them drift away, floating peacefully as a balloon would in the vast sky. Imagine these thoughts and emotions drifting away from you and your bed, enjoying the sensations this brings you. Notice the relief you feel, your body and mind seem lighter and more free now.

Now these anxious thoughts and feelings have drifted far away, completely gone. No longer inn view, as if they never even existed. Now, you don't need to worry about anxiety having so much of an effect over you. You know that if it ever begins to gain control over you again, giving yourself some time and space like you are right now, will give you the relief you deserve.

Just allow yourself to appreciate the calm, serenity of right now. This feeling is like no other you experiance in daily life, and you have created it from the power of your mind alone. If it ever seems that anxiety has taken control over you, keeping you awake at night, feel relief that you can always return to this meditation, where you can release all these negative feelings. This experiance and the relaxing peace it brings to you, is always here if you need. The only thing you need to do is provide yourself the time and space you deserve, so you can feel rejuvenated and refreshed.

Now, we will begin to count down from five to one. With each number we count, you will sink deeper into a state of complete relaxation. Once we reach the number one, you will have drifted off, into a peaceful, refreshing night's sleep, where you will wake refreshed and confident in your abilitites tomorrow morning.

Five. Place your focus with your breath. Fully experience the sensation of your regular pattern of breathing. How with every exhale, tension is carried away from your body. How when your completely connected with breathing you reach another level of peace.

Four. Allow relaxation to take over. Grant yourself this moment, to experiance relaxation alone. Rember all the candles you blew out earlier, and all the tension you blew away. You don't need those feelings of worry and anxiety anymore, so let them stay away. Just focus on yourself and your journey into a deeper sense of relaxation.

Three. Your eyes should be closed now, enjoy the sensation as your eyes are soothed with this relaxing rest. Sink deeper into your bed. Conscious thoughts, like your worries should have drifted away now. Your focus should be alone with the sensations of your body and mind now. Allow other thoughts to float away from you, this is not the time to focus on them.

Two, sink deeper still. Every last muscle within you, feels warm and heavy, feel as they sink deeper into the comfort of your bed. Embrace all it feels like to be completely centred, totally at peace, free from negativity. Your body and mind are free, working together in unison.

One. Drift further into relaxation. Sense wonderful feelings of positivity and harmony, as they wash over you, absorbed by your every last cell. You start to drift into sleep, knowing you deserve this time for rest, recovery and peace.

Drifting off to sleep now, you become fully prepared for tomorrow. You will be able to embrace all the day has to offer, knowing you have complete control over your mind and emotions. This meditation can always be completed again, whenever you feel overwhelmed, struggling to settle into a restful, productive night's sleep. You know you deserve this time to rest, so sink deeper into your bed, enjoying its comfort and slowly drift away, into sleep.

10 Hours Of Guided Meditations For Anxiety, Relaxation & Deep Sleep: Scripts, Affirmations & Hypnosis For Self-Healing, Overcoming Overthinking, Insomnia & Adult Bedtime Stories

By Self-Healing Mindfulness Academy

© Copyright 2021 - All rights reserved.

The content contained within this book may not be reproduced, duplicated or transmitted without direct written permission from the author or the publisher.

Under no circumstances will any blame or legal responsibility be held against the publisher, or author, for any damages, reparation, or monetary loss due to the information contained within this book; either directly or indirectly.

Legal Notice:

This book is copyright protected. This book is only for personal use. You cannot amend, distribute, sell, use, quote or paraphrase any part, or the content within this book, without the consent of the author or publisher.

Disclaimer Notice:

Please note the information contained within this document is for educational and entertainment purposes only. All effort has been executed to present accurate, up to date, and reliable, complete information. No warranties of any kind are declared or implied. Readers acknowledge that the author is not engaging in the rendering of legal, financial, medical or professional advice.

Contents

Daily Meditation 1 (10mns) 85
Daily Meditation 2 (10mns) 87
Daily Meditation 3 (10mns) 89
Daily Meditation 4 (10mns) 92
Daily Meditation 5 (10mns) 94
Daily Meditation 6 (10mns) 96
Daily Meditation 7 (10mns) 98
Daily Meditation 8 (15mns) 100
Daily Meditation 9 (15mns) 102
Daily Meditation 10 (15mns) 104
Daily Meditation 11 (15mns) 107
Daily Meditation 12 (15mns) 109
Daily Meditation 13 (15mns) 112
Daily Meditation 14 (15mns) 115
Daily Meditation 15 (15mns) 117
Daily Meditation 16 (20mns) 120
Daily Meditation 17 (20mns) 124
Daily Meditation 18 (20mns) 130
Daily Meditation 19 (20mns) 134
Daily Meditation 20 (20mns) 138
Daily Meditation 21 (20mns) 140
Daily Meditation 22 (20mns) 144
Daily Meditation 23 (30mns) 147
Daily Meditation 24 (30mns) 152
Daily Meditation 25 (30mns) 156
Daily Meditation 26 (30mns) 160
Daily Meditation 27 (30mns) 165
Daily Meditation 28 (40mns) 170
Daily Meditation 29 (40mns) 176
Daily Meditation 30 (40mns) 182
A Walk Along The Lake - A Bedtime Story (30 Minutes) 189
Guided Sleep Meditation to Relieve Stress and Worry (40 Minutes) 193

Daily Meditation 1 (10mns)

Hello and welcome to your first day in the development of your meditation habit, advancing towards an enhanced, more fulfilling, and meaningful lifestyle. Initially, for the first week, we will perform only a 10-minute meditation, gradually working towards longer sessions, by the end of this 30-day meditation challenge we will be completing 40 minute sessions.

That way, you can ease your way into meditation without feeling overwhelmed.

To begin, get comfortable, so go ahead lay down or sit down in a relaxed position, we will start slow and easy. Comfort is very important for a productive session but we will not be here for long!

Now if you haven't already, close your eyes and take a deep breath. Shift your focus to your breathing, whilst your vision transitions from the light, to darkness.

Take another deep breath and feel how the air flows through your body. Use your stomach to breathe in, which should expand as you inhale. If the rise or expansion is in your chest, then you are breathing from your chest, this breathing is shallow and won't help with your relaxation.

Taking another deep breath, allow yourself to sink deeper into the state of relaxation. Allow yourself to relax and just enjoy the present moment, the peace in the stillness of right now.

First of all, the main focus is on your breath, and little more than breathing deeply. During this session, your mind may wander. If you find this, don't get angry with yourself. Even the most progressed meditation practitioner makes mistakes here. Meditation is about training in awareness and enjoyment of the present, being mindful of your surroundings, and therefore is not an endurance test.

It is a relaxing and enjoyable experience. So, if you find your mind ever wanders, take a deep breath and guide your focus back to your inhalation and exhalation. Maintaining focus will only become easier towards the end of this session. For now, enjoy this peaceful, silence.

This silence, this stillness, is always here. Often, we are just too busy to notice it. Frequently in our fast-paced daily routine we don't take time to appreciate the simple things in life. When we look back to before the internet became so easily accessible, things were taken slow and everyone had to learn to enjoy the simplest things in life.

Today, we find ourselves caught in the cacophony of modern life and we often can't help but be caught in constant hustle and motion. Unfortunately, we frequently fail to take time to notice the little yet beautiful things.

So smile, take another deep breath, as you have allowed yourself to take this moment to appreciate this simple yet beautiful aspect of life.

For now, all you have to do is focus on deep breathing, and the relaxation of your body.

As we approach the end of today's session, take another deep breath and when you are ready, slowly open your eyes and as the light begins to enter, smile.

Feel gratitude flow through you as you have just taken the first step towards the growth of yourself, and a healthy habit of meditation. Thank you, we will see you again tomorrow.

Daily Meditation 2 (10mns)

Hello and welcome back to the second day of this 30-day meditation challenge. To begin, get into a comfortable position and take a deep breath. Now, close your eyes and focus on your breathing.

Throughout the session, comfort remains an importance. So, at any point during your meditation, you start to feel discomfort, feel free to shift your body, to ease yourself back into a comfortable place.

During today's session, continue to breathe deeply throughout. The main theme of the first few sessions will be the continued focus on deep breathing. All you have to do, is breathe deeply and allow your body to absorb the energy from the air.

As you inhale, feel the air enter and expand throughout your body, energizing you. As you exhale, feel the air exiting your body, removing any negative waste. Feel the air flow through your entire body, and feel your body becoming lighter and less weighed down with each breath you take.

Now, you may doubt that air itself has energy. But most likely, taking a deep breath in a stressful situation helps to soothe your mind, helping your feel calmer and in control.

A deep breath allows your body to detach from the chaos of the situation, slow down, and flow at its own pace. It allows you to make more collected decisions, not based on the temporary stresses you face. So, by harnessing the power of a deep breath, we benefit from energizing or even healing properties.

As part of your morning meditation, the aim is to transition to an alert state ready for the day ahead, from a relaxed state of sleep, your breathing helps achieve this. If you don't transition from your relaxed state, you will feel tired and distracted from your focus, preventing you reach the full potential from your day. Thus, taking time to prepare your body through meditation, is essential for the day ahead.

Continue to focus on inhaling and exhaling, deeply. Use this time to appreciate the present moment and that around you. If you are feeling tired, breathing deeply should help energize your body, and help you feel revitalized. Deep breathing and a glass of water are some of the most powerful tools to wake your body.

To remind you, today's session isn't complex. Just focus on your breath, and breathing deeply. Expect your mind to wander during this session, bringing up random thoughts that may make you feel anxious, somber or content.

If so, allow yourself to continue to breathe deeply, giving your body the opportunity to refresh itself as you continue to breathe.

A long day is ahead of you, and accomplishing the most from your day is important. By savoring the peace and simplicity of now, prepares your body for the long day, full of any stress or disorder.

As we draw to the conclusion of today's session, all you need to do is continue to breathe deeply, from your stomach. Whenever you are ready to move forward with your day, begin to slowly let the light into your eyes and smile.

Thank you and have a wonderful day.

Daily Meditation 3 (10mns)

Hello and welcome to the third day of your 30-day meditation challenge. After completing this session, you will have progressed through 10% of the challenge.

So sure, although it has only been three days, remind yourself how far you have come, as you are significantly closer to reaching a habit of meditation, compared to many who give up after the first day. Keep at it, and you will begin to see the changes this will bring to your everyday life.

Now, let's begin today's session. Please get into a comfortable position, whatever you have found works for you, which may be sitting or lying down. All that matters is that you are comfortable before we begin.

Now you are in position, go right ahead and close your eyes. We will start today's session with the focus remaining on deep breathing, although today, this will involve simple breathing exercises. So making sure your inhaling with your stomach and not your chest.

Go ahead and breathe in… And out…

In… And out…

In… And out…

Perfect. Now, on your next inhale, hold your breath for a few seconds before you exhale. Whilst holding your breath, focus on the stillness in the air. Focus on this gentle stillness and let the sense of calmness flow right through you.

So, follow along now and…

Breathe in…

Hold…

And out…

Breathe in...

Hold...

And out...

Breathe in...

Hold...

And out...

Excellent. Continue with this for the next minute.

(Pause 1mn)

Great work. Now allow your breathing to retreat to its natural rhythm. Continue to do this throughout the rest of this session.

Again, you may find your mind begins to wander, which is quite alright. These thoughts may provoke several feelings. Maybe sadness. Maybe happiness. Whatever those thoughts are, remain for a few seconds, then move on.

In this way, by acknowledging their existence for a short while, this may help you understand the cause of those feelings. Maybe an upcoming interview worries you. Perhaps a group reunion feels you with dread. Whatever your situation, these thoughts may help you navigate and overcome those challenges.

Sometimes, in order for you to gain control of your mind, the key is understanding your own thoughts. So, at this moment, rather than immediately pushing your thoughts away, remain with them for a few seconds. Observe them, understand why they cause them feelings inside you, but without getting surrounded and entrapped by your own thoughts and emotions.

Some thoughts may be more direct and incite exactly what you need to stop worrying. So pay attention to these thoughts once in a while, as they can be extremely helpful. Whatever your thoughts may involve, you must never get stuck and therefore overwhelmed with them.

After initially recognizing these thoughts, simply tell yourself that these problems will be addressed after you are finished with today's meditation session, and return your focus back to your deep breathing.

Now, as we draw to the end of today's session. Once you are ready to continue on with your day, simply open your eyes and smile. Thank you and see you again tomorrow.

Daily Meditation 4 (10mns)

Hello and welcome to the fourth day of the 30-day meditation challenge. Now to get started, get into a comfortable position. To prepare your body for its meditation, a time to recharge, and ready you for your filled, busy day ahead, take a deep breath.

Once you are ready, go right ahead and close your eyes. Let your eyelids slowly fall, allowing your vision to transition into darkness, shift your focus to your deep breathing. Today, we will start with the same breathing exercise that we completed in the previous session.

To start, breathe normally at a natural rhythm.

Now, go ahead take a deep breath from your stomach ... In ... And out... excellent.

As the air enters your body, feel how your body starts to feel more energized. The effect of deep breathing in the morning, paired with a glass of water, will help you feel ready for the day ahead.

Now, go ahead and take another deep breath... In... And out... Perfect. With each breath you take, feel your body become more alert and awake. Continue to breathe deeply for the next minute, giving your body the opportunity to absorb all the oxygen it needs to become fully alert.

(Pause 1mn)

Excellent. At this point, expect your mind may get bored and you may find yourself in random thoughts. Again, this is not unusual. Today, despite this, we will not remain in these thoughts. Whenever you find yourself beginning to stray, simply guide your focus back to deep breathing.

Now while we are here, take this time to check in with your physical sensations. Just scan your body, focus on each part of your body, noticing how it feels, recognizing any areas that may feel tense, remembering where they are. Later, we will work on soothing any areas of tension. So, continue to check in with any sensations and how your body is feeling.

(Pause 1mn)

Now, let us work on reducing the number of stresses you may face, starting with relaxing the body. To begin, starting from the top, focus on any areas of tension. To soothe and tranquilize these areas, breathe deeply into that area, imagining the air that you breathe providing the energy to relieve any tension in that area.

Continue to breathe deeply allowing the tension to exit as you exhale, as if your breath is carrying out the tension from your body.

Continue to work your way down your body, check in with each tension, breathe deeply into each, allowing the air to seep deep into that place, so the body can renew and rebuild itself.

Your body has all the knowledge on what it needs to do. All you need to do is breathe deeply. Now, spend a few minutes with your body using this time to soothe and rejuvenate and remove any tension or damage.

(Pause 3mns)

Excellent. At this point you should feel more enhanced. So as we conclude today's meditation. Once ready, slowly open your eyes accepting the light, ready to start the day as a less tense version of yourself. Thank you and see you again tomorrow.

Daily Meditation 5 (10mns)

Hello and welcome to your fifth day of the 30-day meditation challenge. Very soon, as you become more confident and proficient in your meditation habit, we will work on meditating for slightly longer periods of time. For now, today's session will remain short, so as we move forward get comfortable, slowly closing your eyes and shifting your focus to your deep breathing. Now, take a deep breath to prepare your body for this moment, that it is time for its renewal.

For now, continue to breathe deeply. At this point the focus is just to breathe and relax. Allow your body to guide its way through this whole experience. To do this, just relax, observe and don't force anything to happen, but trust in your body.

Now, take a deep breath in… And out…

In… And out…

In… And out…

Perfect. Now, take your time leaning your head from left to right, then back to the left. Feel your neck lighten and become more free as you lean. Now, slowly roll your shoulders in a circular motion forward and back. During this movement feel yours shoulders loosen.

Focus on relaxing your muscles. Remove any tension from your shoulders, back or anywhere else. Just by letting go and relaxing. As you meditate, the release of tension, will only continue as you become more relaxed. Feel how every muscle in your body loosens and becomes more at ease.

Now, focus on your breathing. Observe how your breath flows in and out of your body. Notice how this air flows through your body, how the air enters your lungs, how it relaxes you further. As you exhale, let this air carry out any stresses.

Right now, you do not have to do anything to bring about any change. Just continue to breathe naturally and notice how your body relaxes with each breath. Use this moment to observe the things around you with your mind's eyes. Let your breath gently carry air in and out of your body

Again, your mind may begin to wander. Just take a deep breath, and redirect your focus back to breathing. Initially, you may take notice of these thoughts that pass through. Allow them to pass, without their influence on you.

Observe your breath, how it continues to flow peacefully and deeply, completely effortlessly. During meditation, stress has no place within you. Notice each stage of your breathing. From the inhale… to the pause that follows… the exhale… to the pause before your next breath.

Notice the stillness between each inhale and exhale, feel comfort from this. Envision how the air flows into your nose, and right through to your lungs. Imagine this air brings relaxing energy into your body as you inhale, energizing but also calming you. Whilst you exhale, imagine this air carrying and expelling the stress from your body.

Similarly to your breath, thoughts will come and go. Just like your breath, allow them to enter and leave. Observe each thought for a few seconds, now it is time to be released and exhaled. After that, return your focus back to your breathing.

As you breathe in, observe how the air fills your body tenderly. After you exhale, notice how your lungs deflate leaving them empty, the air carrying out all the worry and stress from your body. Feel your body become more and more relaxed, how calm and gentle your breathing is. We are moving closer to the end of this meditation session. So slowly, it is time to wake your body and mind once more.

For now, let your eyes remain closed, notice the sounds surrounding you. Start to feel what is beneath you or what is supporting your body. Notice your environment, the space around you. Take a deep breath, feel your ribs expand as you inhale. Gently move your shoulders in a circular motion, feeling your muscles stretching once again. Lightly wiggle your fingers and toes.

Now, slowly let the light seep into your eyes and take a deep breath. Gently straighten your back and stretch your arms and legs. You may choose to pause here in this moment and enjoy how calm and peaceful you feel.

Now smile, have gratitude toward yourself that you chose to give this time to care for your body and mind. You may continue with your day. Thank you and see you again tomorrow.

Daily Meditation 6 (10mns)

Hello and welcome to the sixth session in our 30-day meditation challenge. So, go ahead and get into a comfortable position. Close your eyes, gently allow your eyelids to slowly fall, as your vision fades to darkness, take a deep breath. And focus on your breathing.

Now, completely inhale and exhale deeply. To start, we will work on fully relaxing your body. Allow your body to remain still, lengthening and softening your muscles. As done in the past complete a body scan.

Start with your focus on the top of your body, slowly working your way downwards, notice any areas of stress, forcing them to relax if you are holding onto any stress in that area. As you work from your head to your toe, notice any sensations that you feel. For now, all you have to do is release any tension. If you observe any feelings of pain or stress in your body, you need not to do anything yet. Gently pay attention, letting go of any judgement, just be mindful to the messages your body is giving you.

Now, bring your focus to your breathing, notice the depth and pace of each inhale and exhale, and the pause between them. Force your breath to become slower, smoother and deeper. Take a deep breath through your nose… and now a long exhale through your nose. Again, take a deep breath in through your nose… and a long exhale through your mouth.

As your focus remains on your deep breathing, feel the air flow through your body. At this point, its expected your mind may wander, this is quite alright. Today, simply guide it back to your breathing, to this present moment.

For the past few days, maybe you have been pure hustle, maybe you have feeling down, helpless, depressed or stuck in a state of pain. Whatever unfavorable situation you find yourself in, this meditation can help alleviate this pain.

The goal of today's session is to help you better understand your body and mind. You are affirming your body's healing abilities, training your ability to place attention when and where you need.

Meditation is an ancient, powerful tool, helping you to gain complete control of your mind and body. Right now, you are using it to direct your mood and thoughts into a more peaceful yet productive direction. Meditation, has healing powers for your mental and physical health. Your mind is powerful, your thoughts and intentions as potent as medicine. So using meditation as a tool can provoke powerful changes to your life.

Allow yourself to relax further and deeper, with every breath you take. Let the feelings of relaxation and calm spread throughout your body with every inhale. Let the feelings of tension and stress be released with every exhale. Pleasure the sense of peace that washes over you.

Enjoy this moment, spending quality time with your body and mind as it relaxes. This may well be one of the most productive points in your day, rejuvenating you, energizing you and allowing a clear mind, preparing you to complete any task ahead, at ease and to the best of your ability.

Finally, as we come to the end of today's session, slowly open your eyes and smile once again because you have completed yet another session, another positive step toward a more fulfilling life. Thank you and see you again tomorrow.

Daily Meditation 7 (10mns)

Hello and welcome to day 7 of your 30-day meditation journey. Today we will continue with the simple 10-minute session, readying you for an extended session tomorrow, keeping things interesting for you.

To begin, get in your comfortable position, slowly closing your eyes. Take a deep breath through your nose, then slowly out through your mouth.

Breathing from your diaphragm, to soothe the body and mind.

Now, breathe in… And out…

Once more. In… And out…

Again. In… and out…

Now, imagine you are outdoors on a warm, summers day, the sky above you is bright blue dotted occasionally with small white clouds, drifting slowly. Focus on the warmth of the sun, feel that warmth touch you, helping you relax all your muscles.

Allow the soothing sensation of this warmth flow throughout your body, starting from the top of your head down to your toes. Enjoy this warmth calmly take over, relaxing your whole body.

(Pause 2 minutes)

Now imagine that you are walking through a field of fresh, green grass and vibrant flowers. Take a deep breath, smell this nature so it touches your nose, and enter inside you. Smell the beautiful flowers, let them bless you with their gentle yet sweet charm. Feel the foliage tickle your feet as you walk through. Imagine yourself lay down, surrounded and relaxed by this vast field of life, looking up at the sun, as you let its energy wash through you.

As you lay there, notice the wind lazily ripple, imagine now that you are the wind, as it takes you through the field of flowers.

Now, take in a deep breath...

In...

And out...

Feel even more relaxed and rejuvenated as the sun overhead casts a sense of warmth that begins at the top of your head, moves down into your neck and shoulders allowing them to relax completely.

Now, scan your body for any areas of discomfort. As done before start at the top, working down. As you observe any tension, begin to give it a color, a shape, or a texture. Use the power of your mind to visualize and materialize this discomfort.

Now, take a deep breath, notice with each exhale that this discomfort starts to disintegrate, hazily exhaled with each breath you take. As you continue to breath, the discomforts will disperse, feel yourself become lighter and more relaxed and more and more comfortable.

As we come to the conclusion of this meditation, smile, take another deep breath, slowly returning your body to its alert state, fully relaxed and ready for the day ahead. Thank you and see you again tomorrow.

Daily Meditation 8 (15mns)

Hello and welcome to day 8 of our 30-day meditation challenge. Now you are ready to complete a slightly longer session, as we move forward into your healthy habit of meditation.

To begin, simply get into a comfortable position. Then, to prepare your body for its daily meditation, simply take a deep breath. Close your eyes, and as your vision fades from light to dark, shift your focus to your breathing.

Remember, comfort is an important aspect of meditation, so it is okay to change position if you need. Discomfort will cause unnecessary stress disrupting the whole experience.

Now, to begin. Count up to three as you breathe in, hold, and exhale.

Breathe in... One, two, and three...

Hold... One, two, and three...

And out... One, two, and three...

Use your stomach to breathe, as it allows you true deep breathing, filling your lungs completely with air. Whilst you inhale, imagine the air cool, refreshing and relaxing your body as you need. As you exhale, imagine the cool air now warm, the body's stresses mixed inside heating it, as it is carried away from your body. Continue to breathe in this way for the next couple minutes.

(Pause 2mns)

At this point, your body should feel more energized, yet remaining calm and relaxed. With these feelings your systems are activating, preparing you for the day ahead.

Now, allow your breathing to return to its original rhythm. To do this, you don't have to do much. Just give your body permission to lead and guide you through this session. Once you want to return to your normal rhythm, simply tell your body so. It knows the most effective and natural way to bring air in for itself.

Use your breathing as an anchor so you remain in this present moment. Focus on your breath and enjoy the relaxation and peace this meditation brings, for another minute or so.

(Pause for 1mn)

Now, let's do a quick body scan. Start from the top of the head, working slowly down, until you reach the tip of the toes. Focus on any areas that feel tense or uncomfortable. Once you are in an area of tension, simply breathe intently into that area allowing the power of your breath to carry away that discomfort. So, go ahead and do that now.

(Pause 2mns)

At this moment, you may still find some thoughts lingering in your mind. Instead of trying to suppress them. Let them float about in your head, taking note and observing any feelings invoked. Whatever these thoughts, simply acknowledge their existence for a few seconds, before moving on.

As you remain with your breathing, imagine your breath carry in calmness and life force whilst exhaling tension and stress. Continue to breath and feel free to count as you go. All you need to do is enjoy this present moment and the relaxation it brings you.

(Pause for 3mns)

As we are coming toward the end of this meditation, slowly open your mind to your surroundings, open your eyes. Smile as you have given yourself the time to soothe your body and mind. Enjoy your day. Thank you and see you again tomorrow.

Daily Meditation 9 (15mns)

Hello and welcome to the ninth day of your 30-day meditation journey. Today, you become closer to achieving a more fulfilling, enhanced lifestyle, through the enlightening experience of meditation.

To begin, please get comfortable in whatever position works for you. Again, comfort is key for a productive meditation session. Now to prepare your body for this time, slowly close your eyes, take a deep breath allowing your body to unwind and relax.

Breathing In... And out...

Perfect. Again... In... And out...

Once more... In... And out...

In this session, over the next few minutes, you will embark on the path towards a deep state of relaxation. There your body and mind will experience a powerful calmness and meditative state. Right now, this time is for you and only you. All you need to do is allow yourself this moment and just relax. This is your time, and you are in complete control, so you can return to an awakened state whenever you wish. To leave this meditation session, simply open your eyes once more

Now, inhale deeply and exhale fully.

Breathe in deeply...

And exhale fully...

Allow the sound of your breathing to soothe and calm your mind and soul.

Breathe in deeply...

And exhale fully...

Today, at this point, your minds focus may try to leave you, focusing on the internal chatter. Again, this is an expected occurrence, and not a failure. As you listen to your breathing, these thoughts will begin to quiet down once more

Listen to your inhale, gently you will find your mind begin to quiet down.

So, breathe in deeply, allowing the cool, refreshing air to enter.

And exhale fully, pushing out hot, tense air from inside you.

At this point, deeply breathing should stimulate your body, gradually becoming more energized, refreshed yet also relaxed. You may notice this as you allow the sound of your own breathing to wash over you, soothing your very soul, as it brings in the vast positive air, and widens throughout your body.

Whilst your alone with your breathing, acquaintance yourself with the total peace of your surroundings. Now as you journey to a state of deep relaxation, take 5 conscious and deep breaths. As your do, feel yourself to reach a sense of complete and wonderful relaxation.

In… And out…

In… And out… Just allow the sound of your own breathing to calm the mind…

In… And out… Deeply relaxed now…

In… And out…

In… And out… Your mind is at peace.

Take another deep breath, feel this pleasurable sense of deep relaxation. Allow your breath to deliver relaxation to your whole body. Give yourself the opportunity to appreciate this moment, and sensational experience.

As we come to the conclusion of today's meditation, feel free to remain here for as long as you like. Once ready to rejoin your day, simply take a deep breath and slowly open your eyes.

Thank you and we will see you again tomorrow.

Daily Meditation 10 (15mns)

Hello and welcome to day 10 of your 30-day meditation journey. Congratulations! At this point, you have made it through a third of this challenge. You are already well on your way towards the development of a habit and love for meditation, beginning to receive all the benefits it brings. You have already progressed more, than 90% of people who attempted meditation but ultimately gave up.

So to continue with this, let us get started right away. Simply place yourself into a comfortable position, whatever you have found works. Just as long as you are comfortable we can proceed.

Throughout the session, comfort remains important, so keep this in mind and feel free to change positions at any point. We don't want to allow discomfort to ruin the experience, preventing you remove any feelings of stress.

So, if you haven't already, take the final steps to prepare your body for this session, close your eyes and focus on your own breathing.

To begin, we will start with some simple breathing exercises. Using your stomach, inhale deeply and then breathe out. Allow the cool, refreshing air to flow right through your nose, fill your lungs then flow back out your nose.

In… Slowly… And out…

In… And out…

In… And out…

Perfect. Now, let us check in with the body. Although you have just woken, you may still have stress or tension in your body, that remained unaddressed from yesterday. We want to maximize the performance of the day ahead, so we will liberate both the body and mind from this negative energy.

So now, take a moment to perform a body scan throughout your body. Start with your focus on the top of your head, look for any signs of stress or tension in your body. Work your way down to the tips of your toes. For now, simply observing for any signs of stress or tension. So, take a couple of minutes to do this right now.

(Pause 2mns)

Now, imagine that the air that surrounds you, the air that you breath in, has healing properties that your body desires. Let us imagine that it's a colour. Let's give it a bright gold colour, this radiant colour of healing represents the healing power in the air that surrounds you. Now take a deep breath, imagine as you take all that air into your lungs, all that healing energy is taken in as well, right into your body.

As you breathe, feel your body gently start to glow in that colour. See with your mind eyes that with each breath you take your body starts to glow radiantly. Feel your body shine brighter as you take in more energizing, healing air into your body.

At this point in the session you may find your mind to wander. Again, this is expected and not the end of the world. Simply take another deep breath using it to anchor your focus to this present moment. Enjoy the powerful energy the air your breathing in brings to you. Remain with your breath for the next couple of minutes, allow it to energize your body and mind, whilst removing any stress and tension inside you from your exhale.

(Pause 1mn)

At this point, your body should begin to feel lighter and more liberated. Liberated from any stress and tension that were growing inside you. Your mind feels refreshed and clearer. This is the power of meditation. It gives your body and mind the tools necessary to cleanse, relive itself from any tensions and stress it accumulated yesterday. Allow yourself to feel more and more relaxed and you continue to breathe deeply and slowly. Now just as before, continue breathe In… Slowly… And out…

(Pause for 2mns)

Now, from the observed tense areas from earlier, note any areas that are still uncomfortable or tense. There may also be lingering thoughts in your mind as well. Rather than suppress them, let them float about in your head. Take not and observe these thoughts, but never dwell or get stuck inside them. Simply acknowledge their presence and move on with the session.

From here, focus on the tense muscles or negative thoughts, start to use the airs healing energy breathing into these areas, sweeping this negative energy away. Imagine your breath carrying in relaxation and life force, and your breathing removing any stresses from you. Continue to breathe deeply with yourself, allowing yourself to be overcome with relaxation.

(Pause for 1mn)

Now, we are near the end of today's session. Take this moment to have gratitude for yourself, for making the time today to rejuvenate your mind and body, preparing you for the day ahead. Thank yourself for the gift of meditation today.

Once you are ready to return to your day, take a deep breath and slowly open your eyes. Thank you, have a nice day and see you again tomorrow.

Daily Meditation 11 (15mns)

Hello and welcome to day 11 of your 30-day meditation challenge. Now let us get started straight away, so get into a comfortable position, close your eyes and slowly let your vision fade into darkness.

It is time to prepare your body and mind for today's meditation, so take a deep breath. Today we will include something a little new, but for now, let us check in with our current physical body and mental state.

To start, let us relax the body. So first of all, simply check in with yourself. Although you have just woken up, your body may still be holding onto yesterday's stresses. So we will work on relieving the body of these burdens that may well hinder the progress of our day.

To begin this process, we will start with a simple body scan. So, like the last session work down your body, using your focus to scan and observe any tensions.

To change any discomforts, you may be experiencing, you do not have to do anything. However, if any stresses or tensions become too much to observe that they distract you from the session, simply shift your body in position, or in mind, to ease that discomfort. For now, scan through your body looking for these signs of discomfort simply observing them. Go ahead and spend the next few minutes doing so.

(Pause 3mns)

Now, let us work on these areas of discomfort. To start, focus on the area you feel your body is holding on to the most stress. Focusing on this area, imagine it as a shape. So, let's say that the stress in your body is a pointy red triangle, that pokes at your muscles, causing you discomfort.

Now take a deep breath, as you do feel the air from your breath penetrate that area, allow it to gently erode the corners of that triangle. With your every breath, feel the air dull the edges of that sharp shape. Feel that triangle, that tension and stress, slowly melt away with the power of your breathing alone. Remain with your breath now, continuing to work on any areas of tension, melting away those shapes and stresses.

(Pause 2mns)

Now, your body should be relived from all pain, and you should feel very liberated and relaxed from all stress. Next, let us work on relaxing the mind to feel the same way. At this point, your mind may begin to wander. This time, we will allow this background chatter and you simply should remain with these thoughts.

Now, view yourself as an observer, so remaining fair enough away from these thoughts that you are not caught in the emotions they bring. Study these thoughts individually for a few seconds, why they are there, what they may be trying to tell you, but without judgement. So, use this moment to let the mind vocalize with you all it has to say.

(Pause 2mns)

Now, remaining right here, let us take the mind on a quick vacation. Use the power of your imagination, picture a place that would make you feel safe and at peace. This mythical place can be real or completely fictitious. Rather than using all your energy to come up with such a place, sit back and allow your mind to conjure such a place for you.

Using this magical place, take the time right now to explore it. Experience all of the wonderful senses this place has to offer, wander around allowing your mind to take you where it needs, let all your worries and stresses be washed away by the power of your breath.

(Pause 2mns)

As we come to close today's session, you may remain in this magical place for as long as you like, until both your mind and body are free from stress. Whenever you are ready to return to your day, simply take a deep breath, slowly open your eyes and smile.

Thank you and see you again tomorrow.

Daily Meditation 12 (15mns)

Hello and welcome to day 12 of your 30-day meditation challenge. To begin, get into whatever position is comfortable, placing your arms and legs however you like, just as long as you are comfortable.

If you haven't done so already, take a deep breath and close your eyes, readying your body for today's meditation. As your vision fades into darkness, shift your focus to your breathing, and take another deep breath.

We will begin with a simple breathing exercise So using your stomach, breath in through your nose, and out through your mouth.

In… And out…

In… And out…

In… And out…

Excellent. Now, on your next inhale, take a few seconds holding the air at the top, before breathing out again. So, go ahead and take a deep breath in through your nose now… Hold it at the top for a few seconds… Now slowly let it back out through your mouth…

Perfect. Now, continue to breathe in this way for the next minute, allowing the body to unwind and relax itself.

(Pause 1mn)

Next we will cleanse your body from any tensions from the day before. Shift your focus to the top of your head, use your mind's eye to focus on your forehead. Are you holding any tension in your forehead? If so, focus intently into that specific area, allowing your breath to release any buildup of tension you may have found in that area. Now, focus on your brows, is any tension being held there? If so, again use your breath to lift all tension in that area. What about your eyelids? Are they being held tightly shut or are they simply resting closed? If your eyes are being squeezed shut, take a deep breath and let go, allow your body to be calmed, simply allowing your eyelids to lay completely relaxed.

Continue to work through every part of your face, your lips, tongue cheek, chin and jaw making sure each is relaxed as you move onwards.

Now once you are ready, move slowly down your neck, then shoulders. Are you holding these areas neutrally? Or are they being held in an unnatural position? Take a deep breath, let go any tension feel yourself becoming more relaxed allowing your arms to hang peacefully from the shoulders.

Continue slowly scanning your body, focus on each and every area searching for any areas that are tense or are in stress. As you slowly work your focus downwards, continue to note and area of tension.

Move now towards the centre of the body. Observe how your chest feels, then move towards the level of the stomach, now note how this part feels. Keep observing your body's physical state as you shift your focus lower and lower.

Reaching the next level of your hips, continue to observe and once ready keep moving on downwards. Continue in this depth, asking yourself, how do I feel in this area? Notice any tension in this part of your body but without trying to change anything, allow the power of your breath to return this area to a relaxed state.

As you to continue to perform your body scan, right down to the tip of your toes, focus on finding even the smallest amount of tension. Allow your breath alone to soothe these areas, trusting in your body and mind to guide you where it needs.

At this point into the session and your journey with meditation, you should have started to have an understanding on how powerful the tool of meditation is. It grants you the ability to more effectively direct your thoughts in a productive and peaceful direction. This ability brings a profound healing power for both your mental and physical wellbeing. So it is important to remind yourself what a powerful thing your thoughts and intentions are, potent as any medicine.

In this moment, your mind may become distracted and begin to wander. This is fine and expected. Right now, we will take some time to address these thoughts. Allow your mind to wander slightly but without getting caught in the emotions these thoughts may bring. Becoming too attached to particular outcome or an expectation can often lead to frustration and disappointment with reality.

So now, spend time with your thoughts, viewing them from an observer's perspective, preventing you dwell in them for longer than a few seconds. Give your mind the opportunity to say what it needs, for now.

(Pause 2mns)

Now take another deep breath, image the air bring in peace and tranquility. As your breath out, imagine all negativity flow right out of you. Stay focused on your breathing, allowing it to energize and revitalize your body.

With every inhale and exhale, feel yourself become more and more relaxed. You are in complete peace. You are free from worry and stress. You are perfect.

Now, as we come to the conclusion of today's session, you may remain in this magical state of complete peace for as long as you wish. Whenever you are ready to return to your day, in the outside world, simply take a deep breath, slowly open your eyes and smile.

Thank you and see you again tomorrow.

Daily Meditation 13 (15mns)

Hello and welcome to day 13 of your 30-day meditation journey. Now let us begin. Get started by getting in a comfortable position. Feel free to place your arms and legs however you like, so long as you are comfortable. After all, comfort is key for a productive meditation session.

Now to prepare you for this time of relaxation, time simply just for you. Go ahead and gently close your eyes and shift your focus to your breathing. This time is for your personal rejuvenation. Enjoy this little moment for yourself, just take a deep breath and relax.

Now, with your next inhale, hold the air at the top for a few seconds before you exhale. As you do this, focus on the stillness of the air in between your inhale and exhale. Focus on the air's quietude, allowing peace and calmness wash over you.

Continue this focus and breathing for the next minute or so.

(Pause 1mn)

Now, allow your breathing to return to its natural rhythm. We will use this time to relax the body and mind further. Refreshing and readying yourself, preparing you for the day ahead, in a clearer state of mind.

So, let's work towards a complete state of peace within ourselves by performing our quick body scan. First focus on your forehead and look for any tension being held in that area. Next, slowly shift your focus down through your body, simply observing any signs of stress that your body is holding onto. At this point, all you need to do, is notice where any tension is.

So, returning your focus to the gentle stillness between each breath, let us give it substance. So imagine this stillness as a colour, allowing you to see its fullness. Now imagine that colour, this auras gentle magical power, glowing at the centre of your being, right in your heart.

Now, with your next breath, allow this aura to spread, slowly throughout your body. Continue to breath as you normally do, but as you do so, feel this aura spread from your head reaching every point in your body.

All you need to do, is relax and let this aura slowly spread. Welcome this gentle calmness enter all your being. Allow your body this moment to just relax and be still. As this aura spreads, feel it seep deep into you, entering your every cell, every fibre of your being, and along with it accept these feelings of relaxation this magical aura brings.

Allow any areas of tension be washed away, fading with each breath, as these new feelings of relaxation replace them. As you exhale, feel your warm breath weighed down by all that tension from your body, be carried away. Out... And right away from you... Feel your body becoming lighter, and free from tension.

Now, at this point in the session your mind may begin to wader, shifting random thoughts into focus. Some of them may evoke feelings of happiness, whilst others may upset you. So whatever these thoughts may be, this mental chatter will only disrupt your mental tranquility. So today when your mind begins to wander, simply guide your focus back to your deep breathing.

So, breathe in deeply and exhale slowly.

Breathe in deeply...

And exhale slowly...

Allow the sound of your breathing to soothe and calm your mind and soul.

Breathe in deeply...

And exhale slowly...

At this point, the mental chatters should begin to fade. So, continue to focus on your breathing, and your mind will become quieter and quieter. So, once again inhale deeply, allowing that cool refreshing air to seep right into you.

Breathe in... Taking in all that relaxation...

Now, breathe out... Releasing all that stress and tension...

As you focus on your breathing, allow this sound and infinite source of energy soothe your soul, feeling your body start to loosen up becoming more refreshed as you do so. Through your deep breathing alone, allow yourself to become one with your surroundings, in total peace.

Now, as you become more and more relaxed, start counting down from five to zero.

With each number you count, you will feel more and more at peace until you reach a complete and wonderful state of deep relaxation.

5... feeling more relaxed...

4... allowing the sound of your breath calm your mind...

3... relaxation seeps into your all,

2... so deeply relaxed...

1... your mind is now calm.

0... feel the amazing state of deep relaxation

As we come to the conclusion of today's session, allow the sound of your breathing to continue relaxing your whole body, take your time to enjoy this wonderful experience. You can remain in this deeply relaxed state for as long as you like. Once ready, slowly open your eyes and smile as you now have completed yet another meditation session. Thank you and see you again tomorrow.

Daily Meditation 14 (15mns)

Hello and welcome to day 14 of your 30-day meditation journey. To begin, get comfortable in whichever way works for you. You will be here for a while, so make sure you're comfortable as you want to have your complete attention throughout the session.

Once you are perfectly settled in, go ahead, close your eyes and take a deep breath. Shifting your focus to how the air flows in and out of your body. Prepare your mind for this time of rejuvenation, readying you for the day ahead, by taking another deep breath.

So, take another deep breath, let your arms hang lightly from your shoulder sockets, feel the tips of your fingers wherever they may be. Are they touching your leg? Or are they touching a chair or the floor? Whatever your fingers may be touching, feel your fingers and arms hang gently from their sockets.

So, taking a deep breath, notice how you feel, how safe you feel in this moment. Noticing that little bit of gladness in your heart.

Now imagine this journey of relaxation, as a short boat trip. Inhale this fresh, ocean air to the top of the belly, then the middle of the belly. As you do this allow yourself to receive all the trust that you need. Take a slow, gentle breath and feel this crisp air pass down your throat. Feel it reach the sides of your chest as they gently expand with your soft exhale.

Completing this inhale and exhale cycle, allow yourself to receive all the safety and security you need. With your exhale, feel any stresses, anger, fear or discomforts completely withdraw from you, released into the endless ocean.

Now complete a three-part inhale. Inhaling into the bottom of your belly, inhaling through the middle of your belly and straight through into the tops of the lungs. In doing so, you will have received all of the hope, joy and peace you require. Now as you exhale, feel all the sadness, loneliness and grief, gently leave you and the boat you stand on completely. Inhaling right into the bottom of your belly, the middle of your belly and straight into the tops of your lungs, allow this fresh air to seep completely into you.

Inhale, receiving all the healing properties from the air that you need. Exhale, releasing any fatigue, tensions and stresses that you may be holding onto. Take another breath to receive whatever more you may need. Now, for your final breath, inhale deeply from the bottom of the belly, the middle of the belly and finally the top of the belly, so whatever you may need is bursting inside you.

As you release this air with your next exhale, trust that you have received exactly what you need in the perfect proportion, and in a form you can readily and perfectly use it right away, whenever you may require.

Now take a gentle inhale and exhale, notice the boat you stand on has started to move once more. As you slowly glide across this calm, peaceful ocean, notice the boat is nearing right where you began this journey. As the boat bumps into the pier, and you depart back onto solid ground, you feel completely relaxed. Appreciate this boat trip for all the powerful energy you have absorbed, but also all the negative energy you released into the vast ocean.

As you stand before the ocean, notice any pain and tension you had before is gone. Relish the happiness and excitement you feel as your back and shoulders feel relaxed and lighter yet straighter and stronger. Notice your hips feel open and supported, your legs feel liberated from the weight of any tension which has now been released.

Take a relaxed inhale and gentle exhale, pay attention to your fingertips, where they are, on your legs or at your sides. Now, notice your shoulders and arms, how your arms hang freely, full of stability from their shoulders.

You are now fully relaxed and refreshed. So as we near the end of today's session, feel free to remain here for as long as you like. When you are ready to return, take another deep breath and slowly open your eyes. Smile, appreciate yourself, that you have taken this time to rejuvenate your body ready for your day. Thank you and see you again tomorrow.

Daily Meditation 15 (15mns)

Hello and welcome to day 15 of your 30-day meditation challenge. Congratulations! So far, you have already made it to half way through the challenge. Many have tried and failed to make it this far. This means you only have to push for only another 2 more weeks to complete the end of the challenge.

More importantly, as you come closer to forming your new healthy habit of meditation, you may have started to see the benefits of meditation within yourself. These benefits, may take a while for you to truly see they are there. You can only reap those benefits by practicing patience, trusting in the process, both of which are an integral part of meditation.

So, let us wait no further, and get started. To begin get comfortable in whatever position you wish, although sitting upright, in a cross-legged position often works best. Place your hands, palms facing the floor or again whatever is most comfortable for you.

Now, it is time to shift your focus to your breathing. Start with a nice deep breath, to calm and relax the body, ready for the session ahead. Inhale deeply, in through your nose, gently filling your lungs, slowly exhale through your mouth as if your trying to fog up a mirror with your breath. Notice the sound of your breathing, of your exhale. As you exhale feel the warm air exiting your body, as you inhale feel how the air flows right through you. Feel that cool air enter your body, refreshing, energizing and relaxing your body with each breath. Keep breathing in this way for the next minute or so.

(Pause 1mn)

As typical for this point in the session, your mind may start to wander generating mindless chatter. We will address this slightly differently from normal, by allowing the mind to wander for a bit. Grant your mind this time and space so it can vocalize all it needs.

Remember to act as an observer to these thoughts, never getting caught in the emotions they bring, negative expectations or a particular outcome. Becoming too attached in this way, will often lead only to disappointment and frustration with the way things are. So carefully, spend time with your thoughts now, without dwelling on a thought for longer than a few seconds.

(Pause 2mns)

The focus of today's session is releasing what may be bothering us, what's painful or simply what's not working for us. Once achieving this, we can reconnect with our true selves, and our inner essence of peace and tranquility. To do this, with intention and trust chant: "I release and let go," to yourself several time throughout the session.

Now imagine you are standing on a pier, facing a vast sea with no end in sight. Directly in front of you stands a boat, waiting to depart. Imagine placing all your worries, frustrations, struggles, anything negative on that boat. It is about to float into the vast ocean, allow it to take all your troubles with it. The boat may be small, but it can carry all of your troubles, allow this boat to take even the tiniest of tensions far from you, out of sight and out of mind.

Watch as the boat floats away, say to yourself: "I release and let go."

You can say this silently or as loud as you wish.

"I release and let go."

Notice this boat glide easily away, hauling with it, all your negativity, anxieties or simply anything that isn't serving you right now. Allow this boat to leave. Leaving you feeling lighter and free.

"I release and let go."

Continue to breath slowly and deeply. Notice all that negative energy and thoughts vanish from your mind. Freed from the negativity, just allow your body and mind to unwind and relax, preparing them for the day ahead. Spend the next couple of minutes with your breath, simply focusing intently on your breath, and the peace of mind it brings.

(Pause 2mn)

"I release and let go."

Now as we begin to ready ourselves for the day ahead, take another deep breath. Breathe in… And out. Remember that you can use this mantra to find peace and calmness, which can be used throughout the day.

Once you are ready to bring this session to a close, simply take another deep breath, slowly open your eyes. Smile as you have freed yourself from the burden of your negativity. So you are now ready for the day ahead.

Thank you and see you again tomorrow.

Daily Meditation 16 (20mns)

Hello and welcome to day 16 of your 30-day meditation challenge. So let us get started. To begin, simply get into a comfortable position, feel free to lie or sit down, and close your eyes. From there, bring your focus to your breathing and start to feel yourself loosen up. Allow your body and mind to relax...

We will start with a simple breathing exercise. So, go ahead and take a deep breath right now.

In... And out... Perfect.

Now, on your next inhale, breathe through your nose using your stomach, then hold your breath at the top for a few seconds before exhaling. As you hold your breath, pay attention to the perfect stillness in the air.

So, take a deep breath in... Hold... And out...

Perfect. Continue to do this for a couple of minutes. While you breathe in this way, allow your body to uptake the powerful energy from the air yet becoming calm and relaxed.

(Pause 2mns)

At this point, maybe your mind might run astray from the focus of your breath, running away with random thoughts. These thoughts can have the ability to undermine your peace, causing you to be stuck in a perpetual and cruel cycle of negativity, so you become fearful of what is to come in your anticipation of disastrous events. Awareness of these thoughts allows you to change the pattern of your behavior, and thinking, allowing you to overcome this anxiety. So grant yourself the sensation of relaxation, releasing any recurrent thoughts, worry and anxiety about what could be.

In your mind's eye, envision the tip of your nose. Remain actively present in this moment. Allow any thoughts to pass, simply focusing on the here and now. Right now, there is nothing to fear. No worries. Nothing to stress or concern you. For you are just in this moment.

Right here and now, there is just peace and tranquility. Everything in this moment is under your complete control, even your mental state.

So even as your mind begins to wander, you have the power to guide your focus back to your breathing. Disrupt any of these thoughts simply with your breathing alone.

So, if you start to experience any anxiety, uncertainty or simply find yourself starting to drift away, take another deep breath, filling the lungs, reminding you to remain calm in the here-and-now.

In…

And out…

Now, you are ready. Notice your thoughts as they begin to slow. Right now, in this moment, in this space you are completely safe. Controlling your breathing, remaining calm, feel yourself in control.

Now, with your understanding that you are safe and protected and completely in control, use this moment to think about how you feel when you are consumed by your negative thoughts, so allow these feelings to rise.

This may be frightening or even stressful, but know vulnerability is not weakness, and it's okay to feel it sometimes. Right here and now, you are good and safe. A useful trick to calm yourself in the face of fear and anxiety, is simply to recognize it is okay to truly feel these feelings of stress and anxiety.

So, utilize this knowledge, so the next time you feel overwhelmed, anxious, stressed or find yourself dwelling on small details, tell yourself that it is okay to feel this way. It will soon pass.

These feelings will soon pass.

Now, imagine yourself in the future. Envision yourself just 24 hours from now, busy with your day, but haunted by obsessive thoughts and anxiety. You may know exactly what these recurring obsessive thoughts entail.

Maybe you are unsure whether you have locked the door, and can't sit down until you check or maybe you find yourself stressed as the exact ingredients for the smoothie you have everyday aren't in, perhaps you feel the urge to obsessively arrange things or count things in a certain way.

Whatever you may find yourself obsessing over, you do not need to follow through with these negative obsessions. So, imagine these same negative thoughts, but this time remain still, not following through with these obsessions.

If you become consumed by your thoughts surrounding these obsessions, reassure yourself, you did lock that door, you did turn of that light. Continue to reassure yourself, allowing a wave of confidence rush right through you.

You now have no doubts.

Minutes or even hours later, if you feel any doubts starting to creep back inside your head, reassure yourself, you can deal with any stress and anxiety, simply take a deep breath, feeling calmer with every exhale.

Now, take another deep breath, with your mind eye, see the tip of your nose. As you inhale through your nose, feel your lungs fill with air and notice how calmness returns to you. Exhale slowly and deeply…

Now, repeat this a few more times, until you know you are in complete calmness.

(Pause 1 minute)

Trust that you can get through this hard time. Imagine yourself two months from now. Maybe you are enjoying your new habit of meditation and are doing a wonderful job of controlling your now seemingly wild thoughts.

Of course inevitably, you may still experience worry, anxiety and general negativity. However, unlike a few months ago, you are in control of your body and mind, now knowing how to handle this negativity, and with the ability to remain calm, even in the most stressful situations.

You will gain complete control over your thoughts. As the days go on, find yourself becoming more confident and sure of your ability to control your thinking habits. Eventually you'll be a master of your thoughts and able to remain calm at all times.

Whenever your mind begins to bring thoughts of stress, anxiety or just overwhelming thoughts, stop, take a deep breath, and let the air cleanse your body of worry and tension.

Now, picture yourself free of all intrusive, obsessive thoughts and anxiety, living your life free from these problems, and enjoying life at this present moment.

Trust in the power of your breathing, with its ability to overcome the problems you face. Now as we come to the conclusion of today's meditation, once ready to release yourself, take a deep breath, slowly open your eyes. Smile as you now have discovered a new tool for overcoming your problems.

As we come to the end of today's session, have gratitude towards yourself, as you have completed yet another meditation session, and yet another step towards a better, more positive life.

Thank you and see you again tomorrow.

Daily Meditation 17 (20mns)

Hello and welcome to day 17 of your 30-day meditation journey. So, let's get started straight away, by getting comfortable. We will be here for quite a while, so sit or lie down, placing your arms and legs however you may wish, just as long as you are comfortable. Ensuring your as comfortable as possible, maximizes the benefits from this meditation session. Now, if you haven't yet, go ahead take a deep breath, telling your body it is time to unwind and relax. Close your eyes, as your vision fades into darkness, shift your focus to your breath.

Today we will start the session with a body scan exercise. Begin to scan your body observing any tensions but also notice anywhere where you feel a lightness or ease.

So, start from the top of your head, taking the time to work slowly down through every area of your body: your forehead, brows, eyelids, cheeks, lips neck, shoulders, back, every part, until you reach the very tip of your toes. Pay special attention to every area of your body observing how it feels. So, spend the next few minutes with your body now.

(Pause 2mns)

Next, we will check in with your emotions. In the same way as the body scan, simply take a deep breath, and study every corner of your minds state. Observe any feelings, feelings of stress, of happiness, whatever they may be. Allow your mind to wander slightly, helping you understand these emotions and why they are present. So, spend another couple minutes with your mind right now.

(Pause 2mns)

Now, at this point you should have a clearer understanding of the current state of your body and mind. What does it look like today? Are you expecting a day full of obsessive, troubling thoughts? Or do you think that today will be full of clarity and peace? Whatever your current outlook on today, right now we will ensure your state of body and mind are protected.

Now, return your focus back on your breathing. Notice how your chest gently rises and falls with each breath. Notice how the air flows through your body and back out again. Feel the refreshing, powerful air as it fills and deflate your lungs. You may notice that the air doesn't flow smoothly through you, maybe your breaths are shallow or you feel constrained.

So using your stomach, start to take much deeper breaths.

In…

And out…

Now from the chest…

In…

And out…

Now focus on your upper back as you breathe…

In…

And out…

Now, repeat this breathing cycle, but holding the breath before each exhale.

Starting from the belly…

In…

Hold…

And out…

Now, from the chest…

In…

Hold…

And out…

Now, focusing on your upper back…

In…

Hold...

And out...

Breathe deep and slow...

As you continue to breathe deeply, imagine the tension in your body start to release its hold on you. You feel lighter, more refreshed, as if the air is pushing all the tension from inside you. As you breathe, feel this tension fade with every exhale, straight out your nose.

Now, as you breathe, scan your body once more. Notice any tense muscle, tense tissue any tension that still clings on. Breathe intently into these areas, allowing the cool air to soothe these tense muscles or tissues.

At this point now you are in a deeper state of relaxation, you may notice certain areas of tension that you didn't realize before.

So, breathe...

In...

And out...

So let's start with thoroughly deepening the state of relaxation in your entire body. Starting with the back of the neck... in whatever position you're in, feel the air travel through the throat, loosening it, as this air travels to your head notice it become lighter, feel your neck fully supported by itself or by the ground beneath it, not weighed down by worries at all.

Try not to hold any parts of your body in a position, simply relax and let them fall into where is natural. Next, lets relax the shoulders. Again, let them hang loosely.

Let go of the weight on your collarbones and chest, feel your shoulder naturally drawing back as you do so. Work down your arms relaxing each muscle as you go. Notice where your hands are right now, relax them and let your fingers come to rest in their natural curve.

Maintain your deep and slow breathing...

In…

Hold…

And out…

As you continue to breathe, focus on the chest, allow the air as it enters to soothe the tension in that area. Feel your ribs and back becoming lighter and more and more relaxed. Feel yourself wholly supported. Simply let the air carry away any negativity, allowing yourself to be supported by whatever is beneath you. Now, moving on to the abdomen, hips and buttocks, release your hold over these muscles relaxing them. Then, moving down to the thighs, knees and ankles do the same, loosening up these muscles too.

Let them soften as you breathe slowly and deeply…

In…

Hold…

And out…

Finally, shifting your focus to your feet, make sure you aren't holding them in a particular position. Again simply relax, let go, allowing them to return to their natural and most comfortable position.

So, take another deep breath, scanning your body as you do so…

In…

Hold…

And out…

At this point, any tension in your muscles should be gone. Anything remaining will be swept away by the powerful air. What little tension is left, will fade with every exhale.

So, you don't have to do anything right now, simply allow yourself this time to relax. As expected if your mind comes across any emotional stress, just like physical stresses, allow your exhale to carry it right away.

Breathe in...

Hold...

And out...

Let your breath sink deep into you, sending out any unwanted stress. Allow your mind to relax with the sensation of each breath.

In, though the nose.

And out, through the nose.

As you exhale, take a brief moment to double check your body and mind again for any signs of stress. So, once more let's work through the body. Again loosen the muscles of your face and jaw. Inhale slowly, holding this air at the top, and release it smoothly.

Once again, relax your shoulders, abdomen, hips and legs. Feel your body become completely supported by the cushion or group beneath you.

Now, shift your focus back to your breathing, notice where it naturally flows into your body and where it doesn't quite reach. So, feel the air going through your belly, chest, and upper back before you exhale.

Breathe in...

Hold...

And out...

Inhale into the belly, then the chest...

As you continue to breathe in this way, imagine the air swirling all over your body, sweeping up all the tension in your body before carrying it all away, straight out through your nose once more.

As we come to the end of this meditation session, appreciate your body and mind completely free from stress, refreshed and ready for your day. Continue with this deep breathing for as long as you like, but once ready, simply take one final deep breath, open your eyes and smile. Thank you and see you again tomorrow.

Daily Meditation 18 (20mns)

Hello and welcome to day 18 of this 30-day meditation challenge. To begin, let's get comfortable. We will be here for a while, so find whatever position is best for you.

Tell your body it is time to relax and unwind, so if you haven't already, take a deep breath, shifting your focus to your breathing.

Don't let discomfort get in the way of your relaxation, so don't force yourself to stay completely still. Feel free to change your position at any time.

Today, we will begin by relaxing the body. Although you have just woken up, your body may still be holding onto any tensions and stresses from the day before. So, let us begin by starting to refresh your body from these negative energies, starting with a body scan. Start from the top of your head, scanning through your body, simply observing any tension. Notice how your body feels as you do this. Throughout today's meditation, the focus is on relaxing your body and calming your mind.

Now, inhale deeply, taking in all the cool air along with its magical properties, relaxing your body. Slowly exhale, allowing this air to transfer any tensions to outside your body.

As you breathe, your mind may wander, bringing thoughts of your day ahead or yesterday's stresses. Some may remind you of someone or something, provoking feelings of happiness, sadness, or anxiousness

Whatever these thoughts, they are distractive from today's session and its goal. The goal of which, to relax the mind, clearing it from worry. So, to perform your finest today, starting with a clear state of mind is best. In this way, handling your duties and roles will never be easier.

Now, before we delve deeper into this session, take a few moments to dwell on these thoughts. Rather than attempting to push these thoughts far away, focus on them. What are these thoughts trying to tell you? What does your body want you to feel and think? For the next couple minutes, take this time to clear your head by simply thinking where your mind takes you.

(Pause 2mns)

Now is the time to prepare your body for the day before you, refreshing you, so you will feel strong and ready to handle your duties. Right now, you need not do anything. Simply be in the moment. Just think of relaxing both the body and mind. Nothing but calm, relaxing thoughts.

Pay attention to how your body feels.

Where in your body is any current tension stored? Shift your focus to where in your body feels most tense. As you inhale deeply, focus on this specific area of condensed tension. Hold this air leaving time for it to penetrate deep into this tension. Now exhale, allowing the air to carry away this tension.

Next, focus on any other area of tension in your body. Focus on these specific areas as you intently take another deep breath. Breath out with a sigh, letting the air carry away that tension from within you.

Note which areas in your body now feel more relaxed. Imagine this aura of relaxation slowly spread throughout your body with each new breath you take. Let this wonderful aura envelop your body sheltering you from any tension and worry.

As you become more and more calm, feel your attention drift. For the next few minutes, focus on counting, and as you get further along feel yourself reach a deeper state of relaxation. Concentrate your attention on counting from one to ten, as you become more relaxed feel all the tension in your body loosen, allowing your mind to drift into a pleasant place of peace.

Start counting now.

1... Focus on this number.

2... Let the tension be carried out your body, replaced with a deeper state of peace.

3... Now, your more deeply relaxed. Let this calmness fill your body and mind. Just concentrate on the numbers.

4... Image this number in your mind. Relax, relax, relax. Let the tingly healing energy flow through your arms and legs. Feel their heaviness, yet how relaxed they've become. Remain in this pleasant feeling.

5... Drift deeper and deeper, embrace the powerful aura. Let this state of tranquility wash over you. Let the peace enwrap you entirely.

6... Relax...

7... Your body and mind are now embraced in calmness...

8... It feels pleasant and heavy...

9... Let your body drift deeper and deeper, Protected by this aura.

10... You are now wholly relaxed...

Next, you will start to count back from 10 to 1. When you've reach one once again, you will be completely relaxed and at peace, yet also refreshed.

Start to count only when I say start. Slowly counting to yourself whilst I talk. But focusing on only the numbers as I speak.

Start now at 10, focus slowly on each number as you count down. Continue you with each number on your own. With each number feel yourself become yet more deeply relaxed. Feel heavy. Peaceful. Content. Appreciate this warmth.

Relax... Pleasant and calm... Accepting...

Relax... Pleasant and peaceful... At peace with yourself... Soothing...

Relax... Calm and quiet... Deep relaxation ... Tranquil...

Slow, even your breath...

Calm... Warm... Relaxed... Peaceful...

Right now, you are safe. This is your safe space. Nothing can obstruct this peace harming you right here. No mundane worries or stresses can intrude on this space and sense of mental tranquility here. Right now, in this moment is time simply to relax. You have given yourself the opportunity to rejuvenate. Smile, have gratitude as you have allowed yourself this beautiful moment of healing and rejuvenation.

As we move towards the end of today's session, we will count down from 5. As you do so, feel your consciousness slowly return to your body. So take a deep breath now...

5... Slowly returning...

4... Begin to familiarize yourself with your surroundings...

3... Wiggle your toes...

2... Starting to coming back to the outside world now...

1... You are completely relaxed.

This concludes today's session. Enjoy your day feeling refreshed and rejuvenated.

Thank you and see you again tomorrow.

Daily Meditation 19 (20mns)

Hello and welcome to day 19 of your 30-day meditation challenge. To begin, simply get into whatever position you find comfortable and just take a deep breath. Now, consciously give yourself this moment to unwind and relax.

So now, go right ahead and close your eyes, shifting your focus to your breathing as your vision slowly fades to darkness.

To begin, lets us scan your entire body, observing any tensions but also where you may feel lighter and happy.

(Pause 1mn)

Now, let's check in with the mind. Take this time to scan any current emotions that you may be feeling. Pay attention to any feelings of stress, anxiousness but also anything you feel good about.

(Pause 1mn)

Now at this point in the session, your mind may attempt to bring random thoughts into focus, today we won't immediately dismiss them, but observe any thoughts that may arise. Notice if today is good day, if your mind is at peace and quiet. Or, if today is one of them days filled with worry. Simply allow these thoughts to arise. Some thoughts may tell what you need to do with this day. Others may be around what you did yesterday. Whatever these thoughts simply observe them, from a distance preventing these thoughts provoking any feelings inside you.

Now, return your focus to your breathing. Notice how the air flow through your body and then out again. Feel this powerful air fill then deflate your lungs. Feel as your chest gently rises and falls with your every breath.

Again, your mind may wonder once more, bringing random thoughts, provoking different feelings.

Whatever they may be, observe them from a distance, only for a few moments before moving on. Don't allow yourself to get caught in these emotions, as this is only unproductive for this session. Acknowledge these thoughts existence, take a deep breath, using it to anchor yourself to this present moment alone.

Take this moment to observe your breath. You may notice the air not flowing smoothly. Maybe your breaths are weak and shallow. Maybe you feel constrained. Allow yourself to take deeper breaths. So, breathe in now. Hold… and out through the mouth.

Now, repeat this cycle of breathing again but making sure to hold your breath at the top before you exhale. As you breathe, allow the powerful energy in the air to lift away any tension in your physical body. Let it be carried away straight from your nose…

As you inhale once more, scan through your body again recognizing any muscles that may feel tense. Allow your breathing to soothe these muscles. As if the air you let out is filled with any of these unwanted by products of life.

At this point, you may notice areas of tension you did not realize before such as your face. These areas of tension lurk so you can only see them once you are in a deeper state of relaxation…

So, breathe… In… And out…

It is time to start thoroughly relaxing your entire body. All with just your deep breathing. So use the next couple of minutes to focus on intentionally breathing deeply and slowly right now.

(Pause 2mn)

Now, pay attention to your body, make sure you aren't holding any parts of your body in any position… Relax, instead let them fall into their natural resting position. Maintain your deep and slow breathing. As you breathe, feel the air spread through you right through these tensions, soothing and softening these tense muscles.

Next, lets focus on relaxing the feet. Again, make sure you aren't holding them in any position. Simply let them fall to where they naturally desire. Now, take another deep breath, as you do so scanning your body.

Now, at this point most of the tension in your body should be gone, allow any remaining to be swept away by your breath.

Right now, use this moment to intentionally relax. Feel free to continue to note any emotional stresses, that will likely occur in this meditation. Utilize the power of your breathing to release any of these unwanted stresses.

Whilst you exhale, briefly check your body and mind once more for any signs of stress. We will work through the body once more, ensuring your reach a deep refreshing state of relaxation. Shift your focus to your breathing, notice where it flows smoothly and where it doesn't. Imagine your breath floating and whirling throughout your body, sweeping up all that left tension in your body and mind before flowing out your body for evermore. As you continue to breathe in this way, feel your mind clear from any mental chatter, heightening your focus and clarity allowing you to fully sense your entire body.

As you inhale, feel the air bring waves of calmness, clarity and a true sense of well-being. Whilst you hold your breath at the top, let them manifest inside and throughout your body. With each breath you take, you refresh, empower and fortify your body. With each exhale, you release everything that doesn't serve you or your intentions…

Inhale slowly and deeply…

Enjoy this completely unhurried moment. Allowing yourself to completely immerse in the wonders of this meditation, yet giving the body and mind the attention it so desires. Observing and releasing any tensions and stresses, helps energize the body and mind maximizing your performance throughout the day.

By giving yourself this moment of care for just you, is hopefully one of the many self-love activities of your day.

You chose to care for yourself, as you love yourself. You chose to care for you first, so that others can feel your love and care too. Lastly, you chose to care for yourself, as you have the knowledge that you deserve all life's greatness.

So, as we near the end of today's session, smile in gratitude for presenting yourself this beautiful gift. Smile, because you know your true value, that you deserve all the good things in life, and your giving yourself exactly that.

So, once you are ready, take a deep breath, slowly open your eyes allowing them to fill with your surroundings. Have a good day. Thank you and see you again tomorrow.

Daily Meditation 20 (20mns)

Hello and welcome to day 20 of your 30-day meditation challenge. At this point, you have already made it two-thirds of the way through the challenge. Hopefully now, you are feeling very confident and comfortable with this process.

Either way, let us begin right away. Get yourself into whatever position you find comfortable. Take a deep breath and slowly and gently close your eyes. Shift your focus to your breathing. Take a deep breath in, and as you exhale, feel yourself become more relaxed.

Continue to listen and focus on your breathing, relaxing with each breath. With every exhale allow your body to feel soothed becoming more relaxed. More and more at peace…

Slowly take another deep breath, consciously give your body permission to relax. As you breathe remind yourself that this moment is time for your relaxation alone. Allow your body to be completely loose, then once ready we will start with a body scan. Starting from the top of your head, paying close attention to every part of the body, slowly work downwards until you reach the tip of your toes. Simply observe any tensions, allowing your breath to sweep them away. Feel each part of your body becoming looser and free. Notice every muscle, even every muscle fibre relax as you breathe.

Now your completely relaxed, imagine you are in an ideal dream place of calm and relaxation. This place can be anywhere, uniquely yours. You can picture yourself sunbathing in the heat of the sun on a quiet tropical beach listening to the palm trees sway in the gentle wind, or you may imagine standing at the top of an icy mountain looking down at the quiet villages slowly become covered in snow. Imagine yourself wherever you like, just as long as you find yourself at ease in its special, perfect, peacefulness.

Wherever your mind takes you, this could be somewhere you want to go or somewhere you can simply be yourself relish in the calmness it brings you.

Imagine yourself there with your mind's eye, sensing everything your body would sense. As you are in this perfect place, take a moment to experience it with your entire being, filling all of your senses with its glory. Allow the essence of this place to saturate your body with its peacefulness.

(Pause 1mn)

This place is completely yours, a safe haven. Whilst you remain here, no worries or stresses from the outside world can harm you, disturbing your peace. Your body and mind are completely protected here by this peacefulness. So allow yourself to unwind and be calmed in this place. This is a safe space for your body and mind to rejuvenate, preparing This is where your body and mind rejuvenate from this powerful energy.

You are now deeply relaxed and completely at peace with yourself. Focus solely on this place, enjoy your time there now, baking in the feelings of peace, calmness and relaxation.

Remind yourself that this is your place alone, here simply for your relaxation. You are in complete control here so if your mind brings negative thoughts and emotions, simply take a deep breath and feel these thoughts be pushed away. Now is not the time to address any concerns, that is a task for later.

Now, right here is the time and space to energize your body and mind. Allow it to be filled with the energy it needs to repair and heal, improving your functions, preparing you for your day.

As you slowly drift further into a state of deep relaxation assure yourself that you will still remain in control. Assure yourself no matter what, you are in complete control.

With every breath, feel yourself become more and more relaxed, while you experience this continue to focus on listening as I guide you through this session.

Remind yourself that if needed, you can change position so you can remain comfortable. Discomfort will only hinder the benefits of this experience of relaxation.

Now, imagine a sense of calm and peace, spread slowly throughout your body. Release any cares or concerns, letting them float away like bubbles in the wind, until they are no more.

Listen to your body and mind, sense its lack of tension and anxiety. No tensions. No anxieties. You can detect only peace and tranquility. Concentrate on this state of complete calm, acknowledging that you can take this with you throughout your day. Reassure yourself that if your day becomes overwhelmingly chaotic and filled with stress, you can always escape to this place of comfort. This space is always here, no matter the time, through meditation alone.

By harnessing the powers of meditation no stresses can intrude on your mental tranquility. As you can always return to your special place allowing your body to become refreshed rather than overwhelmed.

Finally, you have reached the end of today's session, you can stay here in your special place as long as you like. Once ready take another deep breath and smile. Slowly open your eyes to your surroundings. Enjoy your day. Thank you and see you again tomorrow.

Daily Meditation 21 (20mns)

Hello and welcome to day 21 of your 30-day meditation challenge. Right away, let's begin. So, get yourself in any position, just as long as you are comfortable. Tell yourself that this moment is just for you, allowing yourself to just remain here with your breathing, the silence and peace.

Inhale slowly and deeply from your stomach. Gently close your eyes, allowing your vision to plunge into darkness. As you take another breath, replace your focus with your breathing. You don't have to do anything right now, just trust that your body can let go and relax, as you can't force relaxation, it will simply occur naturally.

Your body may seek healing in an atypical way. Be reassured that your unconscious mind is an expert in healing and balancing any tensions in a safe natural way, while you can carry on with your natural rhythm.

Firstly, we will begin with a quick and simple breathing exercise. Just take a deep breath in through your nose, holding this air at the top for a few seconds, before exhaling. Now, take a deep breath…

In… And out…

In… And out…

In… And out…

Perfect. Now, continue to breathe in this way for the next couple of minutes. Whilst you breathe, focus your mind on this alone, using it to anchor your consciousness here in this moment.

(Pause 2mns)

Continue to be aware of your breathing. Imagine that your inhaling life energy right through the soles of your feet, and as you hold your breath between, this energy circulates throughout your body, before being exhaled out the top of your head. As you breathe enjoy this energy. Simply breathe and relax, relishing in the wonders of this life energy, as it flows through you. Feel a deep sense of comfort as you breathe.

(Pause 1mn)

Now, at this point, you may find your mind start to wander attempting to bring random thoughts in focus. Whatever these thoughts are, and whatever the emotions they may provoke, remind yourself you are in control. Choose to not get caught in these thoughts and emotions, returning your focus to your breathing by taking a deep breath.

Now, notice that your worries, fears and stresses are beginning to crumble in your subconscious mind. With every breath, these feeling will only continue to diminish.

Now, imagine yourself on a clear beach, on a warm summers day with a perfect clear sky. You're here completely alone other than the distant chirps of seagulls. As you walk across the warm glistening sand, feel it slither between your toes. Take a deep breath and as the warm sand massages your feet feel yourself becoming more relaxed.

Smell the salt linger in the air. Listen to the waves gently crashing in. Feel as these sensations give you more energy, refreshing you. Take the next minute to fully immerse yourself in this beautiful place and all it provides to you.

(Pause 1mn)

Now, as you breathe notice each breath synchronize with the waves. As they gently crash into shore, inhale. As they recede, exhale. Move towards the sea, letting the waves wash over your feet.

While you stand here, pay attention to your body and mind. We are going to check in with your body first, so let us do a body scan. Focus from the top of the head, slowly moving down your body observing each and every part. As you work towards the tips of the toes, look for even slight signs of stress. When you come across any tensions, simply breath intentionally in this area, trusting in the power of your breath. So spend the next minute with your body right now.

(Pause 1mn)

Now, it is time to check in with your mind. Again, just notice what sort of state it's in. Is it stressed or relaxed? While your day may have only just began, this doesn't mean your free from negativity. A negative event from any point in your past may choose to affect your mind today. Your mind may be preoccupied by worries in your near future.

You have to do nothing here. Allow your mind to tell you its current state simply by giving it this attention. So spend another minute here remaining with your mind, so it can voice what it needs.

(Pause 1mn)

Now, take another deep breath, returning your focus to the beach, to where you stand, where the waves tickle your toes. Take another deep breath, this time while exhaling push all that negativity out through your feet, letting the waves carry it far away.

Continue to breath in synchronization with the waves, inhaling as the waves roll into shore, exhaling as they push away. As you do this absorb the sea's energy with your inhale, yet pushing away your negativity back out to sea as you exhale. Continue with this for the next couple minutes allowing the waves cleanse and refresh you.

(Pause 2mn)

Now, your clear form all that negativity. As you continue to walk along the beach, allow the waves to gently wash over your feet. Let them wash over you, bringing feelings of calmness.

As you explore this magical place, know you are completely safe to release any of your worries. The sun above you provides radiant light, this energy gleaming all over the beach enveloping you with its peaceful, radiant silence. Seek refuge in this quietness, allowing it flow throughout you, permeating every tissue and cell inside you.

Feel total balance and peace. Allow the relaxing yet energizing essence of this place, flow deeper in you. Feel it be carried right through your bloodstream, allowing every molecule of your body, mind and spirit be touched by this essence. You feel liberated from your usual worries, a deep sense of tranquility taking over you.

You're doing perfectly well. You are in complete control of your body, mind and emotions. You continue to feel improved, harmonious and at peace at all times.

Allow this calmness, this inner peace grow, spread, reproduce in and around your body. As you reach nearer to that deeper sense of relaxation, any worries or negativities you had before, seem calm and quietened for you now.

In contrast, anything that was preventing them positive experiences, seem to give you power and strength. You have the ability to connect with your inner strengths and powers. Whatever your experience with life so far, you are bigger than that. You choose to utilize this opportunity that life gives.

Surprisingly, you feel lighter, liberated and soothed. Now let us continue to walk down this beach. With every footprint you leave behind, it represents any patterns that aren't supportive of your intentions. So trusting in the safety of this place, courageously walk towards your new future, of your full potential

You are doing great, continue to let go now as you walk up the beach. With every step you take, notice yourself become lighter and more free, only making every new step more effortless, the path to your new future couldn't be easier. You are becoming more confident, all that you wanted it getting easier and only more reachable. Any obstacles that used to bother you, just seem to give you more strength.

You feel confident, calmed, and in control, more with each day, as your ability to relax and feel a greater sense of calmness and state of peacefulness grow inside you

Now, we near the conclusion of this meditation. Feel free to remain in this magical place for as long as you wish. Whenever you are ready to return to your day, simply take another deep breath, slowly open your eyes and smile. Thank you and see you again tomorrow.

Daily Meditation 22 (20mns)

Hello and welcome to day 22 of your 30-day meditation challenge. To begin, simply get into a comfortable position. After all, we will be here for quite some time. So have it be laying or sitting down. Whatever you've found works. The only thing that matters is you're your as comfortable as possible, so your focus is solely on this meditation.

So, go right ahead and gently close your eyes. As your vision fades into darkness, prepare the body and mind for this moment by shifting your focus to your breathing. Using your stomach, take a deep breath in. Notice how the air flows throughout your body. Observe the air's gentle flow as you take in its fresh morning energy.

Right now, all you need to do is acknowledging your body and mind, allowing this time for them to refresh. As well as a glass of water this short meditation session has the power to bring your body and mind to an alert state, preparing you for the day ahead. By the end of today's session, you will feel refreshed yet at peace. Your mind clear and focused, and your body energized.

So, take another deep breath, feel the air start to energize your body and mind so they feel more alert. Take another deep breath, simply feel the energy flow into and around your whole body.

To begin, we will start on making the body feel rejuvenated, by performing a quick body scan. Although you may have just woke up, that does not mean your body is completely free form stress. Worries from yesterday may have created tension in the body, or even an uncomfortable, unsuccessful sleep. Either way, let us start your day with a clean slate.

So, starting from the top of your head. Focus and observe any signs of stress in the body. If you notice any signs on tension, with intention, simply breathe deeply into that area, imagine the air flow directly to that area permeating every cell, every molecule, soothing it, removing all the stress, simply through your exhale.

Let go of your body, simply allow it to be naturally supported by the surface beneath you. Slowly move downwards towards your brows, breathe deeply and just let go. Make you aren't holding any area in any particular position, allow them to rest where is natural for them. Now, your eyelids... Breathe deeply and let go... Do not squeeze them tightly shut, but let them fall, resting naturally over your eyes. Move down unclenching the jaw, relaxing your lips and cheeks, ensure your tongue is settled in its natural position. Simply use this time to relax and let go.

Moving down, reaching your neck let go, rather than your mind, allow the neck to support the head finding its natural position alone. Again don't hold any part of the body in any position, your body knows equilibrium. Trust in your body's ability.

Now, shift your focus down to your shoulders... Simply let go, breathing deeply...Relax...move down to the top of your chest now... Feel as your chest gently rises and falls, as you breathe in... And out...

Feel how your back supports your body. Breathe in deeply, allow it to relax and unwind, so it supports your weight effortlessly. Move towards your stomach now... continue to breathe deeply, observing how this rises with you inhale... and fall with your exhale...

Shift your focus to your arms now, let go, allowing your muscles to lengthen and become softer and more free. Simply relax and let go, find your fingers become to rest with their natural curve.

Move down towards your legs now. Breathe deeply and allow these muscles to soften, trust in your body and its ability to relax without your minds control. As you Breathe, welcome the introduction of this relaxing yet refreshing aura as it flows throughout your body.

Now, take this moment to work your way back down through your body once more. See how its free from tensions and stresses, whilst using this state of deeper relaxation to notice any that may remain. Feel as your body becomes free form all its burdens, liberated from all its worries. Notice your body become lighter, yet stronger enjoy the feelings of relaxation this brings. Remain with your breath and relish in these sensations now.

(Pause 2mns)

As expected, we have reached the point in the session where your mind may attempt to take you elsewhere. These thoughts that it brings may cause you to become anxious, or fill you with great happiness. Whatever these thoughts, rather than push them straight away, choose to acknowledge their existence.

While you simply exist in this moment, allow your mind to wander slightly. Allow it to voice all it needs, whilst you simply observe from a distance. Remain with each thought, but only for a few seconds, before you take a deep breath and move on.

Using your breath, anchor yourself to your inhales and exhales so you remain in this moment. Don't attempt to reach any particular thoughts, only let them come to you or simply enjoy the quite nothingness in your mind. Remain with your mind for the next moment or so.

(Pause 1mn)

Now, you will begin to notice your mind become more settled. All your thoughts seem disappear quickly just like a shooting star in the night sky, seen but soon forgotten. Remain alone with your breath now, enjoying the tranquil darkness of your mind.

Here, there is nothing. There is no place safer than right here. Nothing from the outside world can deceive you, taking this opportunity of mental clarity and tranquility from right beneath you.

Just take another deep breath, enjoy the peaceful silence and stillness of right now. Your mind has now been cleansed of all that unproductive waste, and in its place just peace and relaxation. Continue to breathe deeply, allowing your body and mind to absorb the airs simple energy, energy you will need to maximize your performance in the day ahead.

Now, as we come to the conclusion of today's meditation, take a deep breath and smile. Smile in gratitude towards yourself, as you have given yourself this moment simply to rejuvenate. Feel free to remain here as long as you like, but once you are ready, take another deep breath and slowly open your eyes. Enjoy your day. Thank you and See you again tomorrow.

Daily Meditation 23 (30mns)

Hello and welcome to day 23 of your 30-day meditation challenge. Let's get started straight away, so make yourself comfortable in whatever position you like, in your usual meditation location, or anywhere free from distractions. Take a deep breath, whilst consciously giving yourself this time, simply to relax.

Now, gently close your eyes and as your vision fades dark, turn your attention inward, shifting your focus to your breath. Remaining with your natural breathing rhythm, simply observe how the air flows through you. Notice as the cool air passes in through your nose, expanding your lungs.

With each exhale, encourage any tensions you may be holding on to, to become attached to the molecules of this air, and therefore carried away with each breath. Continue to observe your breathing, noticing as you become more relaxed it naturally deepens and slows.

We will start by relaxing the body, so let us perform a simple body scan. Before we start this, give yourself this time and permission to fully let go, allowing the ground beneath you, to fully support you. Savor this moment, and the relaxation and gentle ease it brings to your body.

Today, unlike usual, we will start from the tip of your toes and work our way up towards the top of your head. So, starting at your feet, look for any signs of tension, relax and let go. Move your focus up from your feet and use this next minute to begin to release your ankles, lower legs and knees from any negative energy they are holding onto.

(Pause 1mn)

Feel as each part of your body becomes lighter yet stronger as if connected to the energy around you as you, as you release anything that holds you back.

Unearth a sense of ease in your thighs then hips as you let go. Moving upwards, take a deep breath releasing the forces that hold your lower back stiffly. Continue this process, and as you move on upwards, find yourself increasingly comforted and connected to the collective energy of the universe that surrounds you.

Welcome this sensation of deep relaxation enter your abdomen. Let your chest and arms rest, grounding themselves using the surface below you. Moving forward allow your neck and throat to release both its physical and mental tensions they may be holding onto. Use this next moment to relish in this sensation.

(Pause 1mn)

Now, unclench your jaw and feel the muscles in your cheeks become looser and placid. Notice how your holding your forehead, allow it to soften as you let go, and observe how the rest of your body follows and softens too.

Now, return your breathing to its normal rhythm. Find yourself dive deeper into a state of relaxation. Here, right now, you are completely safe and supported, as you guide yourself through this journey towards a completely calm state of mind.

Now you are feeling more deeply relaxed, we can begin to check in with your current mental state. Just like your body scan we will explore your mind searching for any negativities. What do your feeling look like right now? What is your current state of mind? Here you don't have to do anything, simply sit back and just observe your mind, passing no judgements and allowing it this freedom.

Whilst you continue to meditate, your mind may start to stray, bringing up random thoughts. Like usual, don't immediately suppress these thoughts, but allow them to surface so you can acknowledge their existence. Provide the space in your mind right now, so these thoughts and truths to surface. Whatever these thoughts or emotions, helpful or unproductive, allow them this space temporarily.

Reminisce on any moments that you may have felt stuck or overwhelmed. Take this moment to recognize your current feelings and state of mind. Accept this as only the current feelings in this present moment. Any emotions are true and legitimate. Anything you feel, both the good and bad, is part of your completely unique journey through life.

Let down your guard, break down your walls to this emotion. Right now this space is safe, without judgment but rather acceptance. Often our natural instinct, is to suppress, reject or ignore the existence of difficult emotions. But, by doing so this only brings about more suffering.

Often we may busy ourselves so we can neglect what really needs our attention. Some may fear failure, where even the thought of doing so can overwhelm and completely paralyze them. Others may feel so anxious about what needs addressing they become completely restless.

Whatever emotions you may feel, understand and recognize that it is okay. You may have slipped into a cycle that leads you to feel this way. Your emotions may make you feel down, and although it may be easy to fall into depression, they don't define you. How can something that is always changing define who you are?

Recognize your minds voice. Recognize your true potential, disregarding unrecognized expectations from yourself and others alike, that may have a role in your judgements of yourself. Any aspects that may have a role in any negative talk you may be experiencing, disregard them.

As you begin to understand your thought patterns, and any unproductive cycles you may find yourself stuck in, bring your attention to your own emotions. Study them as a bystander. Observe them without passing judgment or attaching any label to them. All feelings are legitimate, and exist for good reason. They all have a place in highlighting your strengths but also weaknesses.

In order to greaten your understanding of yourself, exploring these feelings and why they exist is great tool to do so. So take this next moment to pause, simply allow these feelings to surface without your judgement.

Acknowledge all feelings, and unlike usual don't push them away. So, use this time now to observe these thoughts and feelings now.

(Pause 1mn)

Simply be in this place. Remain in this moment, right now, in the present. For this meditation to work best this is the way. Continue to open your heart for any feelings that may arise, allowing them to simply exist here.

Resisting the discomfort of negative emotions and therefore this present moment in only normal. Do your best to stay mindful when difficult thoughts may arise, remaining in the present.

Whenever you find yourself trying to avoid this moment and any uncomfortable thoughts, don't act immediately. Instead, take a deep breath, secure a moment where you can just pause, by doing so this gives you the ability to recognize the opportunity to make a different choice. A choice that has the ability to break you out from unhealthy patterns of behavior you are entrapped in.

This little pause is so powerful, providing you the space and time, allowing you to prevent negative habits and behavior from externalizing and becoming your norm. This pause provides you the power to calmly collect your thoughts and respond appropriately, rather than prioritizing the avoidance of these difficult emotions.

The ability to move forward and grow, simply comes with honesty and acceptance. So firstly, recognize the emotion inside you allowing it to exist as it is. Then utilize your curiosity to explore why this feeling, and what lays behind it.

Explore your own truth. Continue to breathe deeply, allow space for these truths to surface. Use this time for some deep self-inquiry, to develop a better understanding of yourself. Ask yourself some questions about what you are experiencing, and what feeling are underneath these experiences.

Whatever you feel, is there a physical component?

You may find yourself without the answers you seek initially and that is okay. Use these next moments of complete quietness, to continue to explore your feelings allowing all to surface.

(Pause 1mn)

Make space for the truth and your acceptance of what is, and with time the answers will simply come to you.

(Pause 1mn)

Now, remain without any judgments. Allow all self-limiting beliefs to vanish. Let go of any expectations, negativity and fears, anything that may be holding you back. It doesn't have to be named specifically, just let go. Let go of all that holds you to these negative feelings and patterns and replace them with positive thoughts and gratitude.

Use this time to release, release all you may have pushed deep down, any anger, fears, resentments, anything that you've tried to ignore.

As these thoughts and feelings are brought to the surface, fill yourself with a sense of deep and powerful love. Truly vision what is really happening, proceeding with care and compassion for yourself. Continue to move out of your typical thinking patterns and into this felt experience using this time to truly care for yourself.

Now, choose to provide yourself this moment offering self-love and kindness. Place your hand on your heart, signaling you to open your heart so it can receive your good intentions and positive energy. Allow this to flow through you, filling your entire being with love and positivity. Only you truly know what you need in this moment, so use this time to care and nurture yourself in this way.

All you need to do is give your mind space, and it will voice all it needs. This answers will come; you simply need to listen. You are in control, all the tools you need are inside you, all you need to calm yourself, and find complete peace is within.

Now, we come to the conclusion of this meditation. So bring your attention back to your physical body and take another deep breath. Feel a rush of energy as it enters back into you, just like a warm wave flowing over you, slowly awakening your body.

Once you're ready, open your eyes, now you are fully in this present moment, feeling awake, refreshed and energized. Thank you, have a nice day and see you again tomorrow.

Daily Meditation 24 (30mns)

Hello and welcome to day 24 of your wonderful 30-day meditation challenge. As usual, begin by getting yourself comfortable. Either sit or lay down, placing your arms and legs wherever you like, just as long as you are comfortable. Comfort is an important aspect of meditation, after all.

Now, go ahead, close your eyes and take a deep breath, preparing your body and mind for this time of relaxation and rejuvenation. As your vision fades into darkness shift your focus to your breathing. Give yourself permission to relax.

Now, take a deep breath... In through the nose...Holding it at the top for a few seconds... And out through your nose once more.

Wonderful. Let's do this a few more times.

In... Hold... And out...

In... Hold... And out...

Perfect.

Take this moment, remind yourself of the importance of this time, and the true impact you can feel, just by removing all stresses as you start your day. While you may have just woke up, there may be a buildup of stresses from the day before, this stress can clutter your mind, causing tension in the body.

With this meditation, you are giving yourself the opportunity to cleanse your body and mind from any stresses and tensions, readying you for your day. Just like a morning shower, your rinsing away all them worldly worries.

Now, take a deep breath, and as you do so start to feel yourself becoming more and more relaxed. Welcome this gentle relaxation, allow it to wrap around you soothing you, just like a warm, fluffy blanket.

Right now, right here, you are safe. This is a completely safe space, away from any harm where you are in control. Take this time, simply to relax, unwind allowing the power of your breath to sweep away any worry and stress. Allow the air to flow through you, flushing out any stresses.

For now, observe any sounds that surround you in your immediate environment. Whatever you hear, allow it to add to your sense of relaxation. As you inhale, feel the fresh air enter, making your body feel more aware, energized and refreshed. As you exhale, allow yourself to release any tensions and stresses it may be holding onto in either your body or mind.

While you continue to meditate, your mind may become distracted, bringing up random thoughts. Remember this is okay and completely natural, so don't become frustrated. Rather than push these thoughts away, acknowledge they exist, after all they may be trying to tell you something important. Just make sure you only remain with these thoughts for a few seconds and not to dwell on them.

Now take a deep breath and move away from these intruding thoughts. Don't attempt to reach any that may appear.

So now, imagine that you are in a dark place. So dark you can't see a thing. Although there is nothing in sight you can sense you are safe here. This dark space is the vastness of your very mind. This dark vastness can be filled with anything, even your thoughts.

Imagine your thoughts lighten the darkness of this place just like starts in the night sky. So, just sit right here, observing each and every thought.

Reach out towards any of these stars of light and inside, you will find a memory or a passing thought. Look up and notice these stars of thought twinkling brightly as you inhale, and fade away while you exhale.

Remain here, enjoying the calmness of this place. As you sit here, observing your thoughts, as a new thought enters, another star brightens the dark sky. Here, you can observe your thoughts from a distance, preventing you get caught in the emotions they may provoke.

Just allow your mind to pass any thoughts it desires, like a shooting start across the night sky. Notice any thoughts as they come as go, shining clearly, before disappearing back into the darkness.

Remain in this space for the next few moments, observing all your thoughts and giving your mind this space to voice all it needs. Only by voicing these thoughts can the mind be fully cleansed and ready to let go of all it doesn't need.

(Pause 2mns)

So, continue to breathe, embracing a sense of calmness spread through your body. Allow your breath to carry away all your worries, thoughts and concerns. With every inhale, embrace this sense of relaxation and wholeheartedly accept this calmness. Take another deep breath, allowing your body to relax, and just let go completely. Allow your body to loosen up, just letting the surface beneath you support you completely.

Now, as you continue to breathe deeply, feel how your mind quietens and calms down. Your train of thoughts begins to slow and your feel yourself becoming ever more relaxed.

Remind yourself that if you begin to feel any discomfort at any point in the session, you can gently move your body to ease that discomfort. After all, discomfort with only hinder the process of relaxation.

Now, simply using the power of your imagination, transform this dark vast space you are in currently, to a place you would feel safe, at peace and completely relaxed. Don't spend much of your energy doing this as your mind knows exactly the place you can feel this way.

This place is your safe haven, with its own unique properties either real or completely fictitious. Whatever the place, all that matters is that your mind can take you there. It may be on a quiet, sunny beach, or the top of a harsh mountain, or even on a lazy Sunday in your own garden.

This place is somewhere you wish to be as it has a sense of peace, nostalgia or even somewhere you associate with a feeling that you now yearn for again. This place is your safe haven, created solely by you.

So, take this next moment to enjoy yourself in this place. Fill your senses with everything here, filling you with peace.

(Pause 1mn)

This magical place has been and is always here, just locked away from your mind. Occasionally you have access to it. When you are in total peace, such as right now, you have this ability to unlock the gate that leads you here.

This place is always here, so you can always come again in future, once you are in total peace. Take all the peace and relaxation from this magical place with you. So if you become overwhelmed, finding yourself stressed or tense you have this reserve of energy that you can use. Whenever you need a break from the chaos of your day or the outside world, this place is always waiting ready for you to come back to.

You find yourself in this beautiful place now. Simply relish in the calm peacefulness of right now. As you wander around this special place, take in all its energy, relaxation, anything it has to offer.

While you are in this place you are completely safe, here no one can disturb you. Trusting in this, allow your body and mind to fully immerse itself here in this place. Notice the magical aura you find yourself surrounded by, allow this energy to seep deep into your mind, body and soul.

With open arms, accept this magical aura as it seeps into your every cell. Simply use this time here to absorb all it energy, so you feel at total peace with yourself. With every inhale, feel yourself become more refreshed and energized, more motivated, more strength and less stressed and tense.

Now, you are deeply relaxed and filled with positive energy. You are completely connected with your body and mind. Continue to focus on your safe haven now, wander round some more allowing yourself to absorb as much of its magical energy as you can. Simply remain here, knowing you are in total peace and tranquility, filling with positive energy. Calm and relaxed.

Here, exists no tension, no anxieties. Focus on its gentle stillness, this gentle calm, you can take with you to the outside world, protecting you from the stresses and chaos of your day. With this power and energy, you continue to absorb from this place, no stress or anxiety can intrude and disturb your mental tranquility.

So, take this moment now to smile, for you have finally discovered this wonderful place. In future, whenever you feel overwhelmed or stressed, know this place awaits your return and is always here when you need.

Maybe you have been working yourself really hard lately. Maybe you have grown tired and sleep is not enough to heal your body and mind. Perhaps you are too harsh with the expectations of yourself. But now, you are choosing to love and support yourself by giving yourself this time and space for your body and mind to truly rejuvenate and repair, so they can perform at their best.

You chose self-care. You know that you are of importance. You know you are worthy of love and you deserve all the good things in life. You trust that you will get to enjoy all the good things in life, after all, it all starts with this meditation.

Now we come to the end of today's session. Feel free to remain in this place here, as long as you like. Remember you can always come back to your magical place, whenever you wish. So, when you are ready take a deep breath and gently open your eyes. Thank you, have a nice day and see you again tomorrow.

Daily Meditation 25 (30mns)

Hello and welcome to day 25 of your enlightening 30-day meditation challenge. To begin, simply get yourself comfortable. Either sit or lay down, whatever you've found works. After all, you will remain here awhile so your comfort remains of importance. Discomfort will only hinder the effects of today's session.

So, if you haven't already, take a deep breath and slowly close your eyes. As your vision fades into darkness, shift your focus to your breath. Take a deep breath now, preparing your body and mind for this time, simply to let go of all worries and stress and let calm seep through you.

So to start, we will perform a quick breathing exercise. Go ahead now, using your stomach take a deep breath. Allow the air to completely fill your lungs, spreading through your body, and then slowly exhale.

Breathe in… And out…

Breathe in… And out…

Breathe in… And out…

Firstly, we will start by relaxing the body. To do so, we will do a quick body scan exercise so we can locate any tensions your body is holding onto, later working on removing them.

Let's go ahead now and place focus at the top of your head. Moving slowly, focus on each and every area in your body scanning for any signs of stress. Start from your forehead, slowly moving down to your brows, your eyelids, nose, cheeks, lips, jaw neck…

Make sure each and every one of these areas aren't being held in any particular position but are at complete rest in their natural position.

Continue moving down to your shoulders, upper chest, lower chest, stomach, back, arms, fingers, pelvis, calves, foot, and finally toes.

Now use these next few moments to scan through your body a few more times, continuing to observe any tensions. Right now, you don't have to do anything with this knowledge. So, simply spend the next couple minutes with your body, observing how every part feels.

(Pause 2mns)

Next, give substance to that pain or stress in your body. So let's view these areas as red-hot. Using your mind's eyes view these areas. See they have an unpleasant, unhealthy glow and tense heat to the touch. Truly envision how unpleasant it is to hold this tension in your body. You don't have to hold onto this tension any longer, because as you relax your body will become free from such pain.

On your inhale, hold your breath at the top for a few seconds, before exhaling once again. While you hold your breath, focus on the gentle stillness the air carries. We will work on introducing this gentle stillness into the body, relaxing you completely.

So, imagine the air you breathe carries a magical aura. Give it any colour that your drawn to. Now, on your next inhale, imagine this magical aura spread through your body starting from your centre - your heart. Feel yourself glow with this colour.

Imagine that this magical aura is like water, in complete abundance, slowly flowing calmly through your body while you continue to breathe. Take this powerful energy, introducing it to your entire body. Allow it to flow, trickling into every cell, so its magical healing powers are completely soaked up.

Now focus on this energy, bringing it into your forehead, then moving down into your brows, eyelids, and then working it through to the rest of your body. Allow this relaxing energy to just take over your entire body, calming you completely. Simply allow your body to be soothed removing all pain.

Continue to breathe deeply, allowing the colour, and magical aura to spread throughout, seeping into any red-hot areas where stress gathers. Continue to breathe, focus on these hot stressed areas, noticing how they start to vanish as you do so.

While you breathe, feel these hot-red areas grow smaller and smaller. It is as if the air you inhale goes exactly to these areas, chipping away at any residues of stress and carrying it out of your body. So, remain here completely alone with your breath for the next few moments, allowing this relaxing energy seep into every cell and every molecule of your being.

(Pause 1mn)

Now, let us check in with your mind. Maybe you are fixated on your worries, worries on the future, worries about yesterday's troubles. These negative thoughts only drive your mind into cloudiness making you feel constrained and muddy.

At this point you may find your mind starts to wander, bringing up random negative thoughts. It is only natural for your mind to wander in this way, so don't beat yourself up for it. Rather than silencing every passing thought, instead choose to observe each one but refusing to get caught in its emotions.

Give permission for yourself to become at ease with each and every thought that passes through your mind, after all they are only passing. Any tension this moment may bring you, caused by a worry or stressor in your life right now will quickly diminish, being reduced from excessive amounts to a reasonable place.

Truly see what you give meaning to, before manifesting it into your body. You are not the manifestation of your worrying thoughts, so dismiss them, they are unwanted and unneeded here. Reject these worrying thoughts with positive self-love that only nourishes your body and mind, as you are worth the good things in life.

As you move forward, continuing to let go of all negatives that hide inside you, find yourself becoming calmer, relaxed and in complete peace.

Allow yourself to gently sink deeper into a state of calm and relaxation. Trust that you are in total control of today's session, that you have the power to go deeper, deeper into a state of complete calm, where no sounds from the outside world can impede, no light except that of positivity that shines within, and the feeling of touch that is soft and of comfort.

At rest, breathing slowly and deeply, just let go. Feel the touch of the surface that supports you, begin to fade away. The only sensations you sense are of your own vibrations and your internal energy.

Feel as everything inside you becomes replaced with a positive and healing feeling of inner peace. Feel as your thoughts and every cycle within you, gently quieten as they simply run on this positive energy. Feel as your body replenishes itself with this energy, replacing anything that holds you back from your true intentions.

Feel the soothing vibration of positivity grow around your whole being. You may envision its distant colour glow behind your eyelids or feel tingling in your hands and toes as it spreads. You may notice your body becoming warmer and slightly heavier with each breath, every inhalation of this magical air sending you deeper into a space of soothing relaxation. Allow yourself to feel a deep, boundless sense of relief seep into every corner of your mind.

Grant this air the power to heal any bad negative feelings you have of yourself. Right here, in this moment and moving forwards, only positive thoughts may reach you allowing you to drift heavier into this warm, refreshing sense of deep relaxation.

Now, you have made significant progress with this challenge. Within the next 5 days, you will have completed this journey with me, although hopefully not your journey with meditation altogether. Even though you may only experience yourself very new to this experience, you may have found meditation just gets easier and easier. You may have found that reaching that relaxed and refreshed stare is only becoming more natural for you.

You have chosen yourself. You have given yourself this time to rejuvenate and relax, as you understand the importance of caring for your mind, body and soul. You see the beauty of this peaceful tranquility.

You understand the importance of caring for yourself, so you can receive all the good things in life, that you know you deserve. Through working hard, you will get all those beautiful things in life, and you know to do just that a stress-free body and mind filled with clarity is so important. Right now you are caring for yourself to achieve just that.

You love yourself, so you chose to care for yourself. Meditation is one of many self- love acts, so you chose to treat yourself to this gift. You may have been working yourself hard, and without this break to simply relax and rejuvenate you will burn out.

With a body and mind that is cared for, you are capable of achieving anything you desire. You know your own abilities that you can get anything you want out of them. With a refreshed and energetic body and clear state of mind, you best is enhanced.

Now, take another deep breath and smile, for you are grateful for yourself, as you have chosen to care for yourself. Continue to breathe deeply in this way, taking in all that energy your body needs to rejuvenate and be prepared for the day ahead of you.

Now, as we come to the conclusion of today's session, feel free to remain here simply with your breath, just relaxing as long as you like. Whenever you are ready to return to your day, simply take a deep breath and slowly open your eyes. Enjoy your day. Thank you and see you again tomorrow.

Daily Meditation 26 (30mns)

Hello and welcome to day 26 of your 30-day meditation journey. So let us begin straight away, by simply getting comfortable. Whether you are sitting or lying down the only thing that matters is that you are as comfortable as possible to maximize the effects of today's session.

Now, take a deep breath, completely give yourself this time to just relax and become energized, ready for your day ahead. Today, you don't have to begin by closing your eyes just yet. For now, just listen and allow your eyes and mind to completely wander as they please.

and give yourself permission to just relax and energize for the day ahead. Right now, you do not have to close your eyes yet. In fact, you can just listen and allow your eyes and mind to wander as they please for now.

Now we will begin to relax the body and mind. Using your stomach, breath in slowly and deeply, on your exhale, close your eyes and when you breathe in again, gently open them once again.

Breathe in... And out...

Repeat this cycle of breathing a few more times, opening and closing your eyes with each new breath.

(Pause 1mn)

With every exhale, as you close your eyes, feel your eyelids becoming heavier as you start to feel more and more relaxed. Breathe in and out... Start to form a peaceful, rhythmic pattern with your breath.

Breathing in... Eyes open...

Then breathing out... Closing your eyelids...

As you inhale, feel as a warm soothing energy begins to flow inside you. With every breath this warm energy is carried in, slowly moving throughout your body. Take in this energy, feeling pure comfort as your muscles lengthen and relax as they let go.

Your body is becoming heavier and heavier, falling deeper and further into relaxation. As your body uses this energy to sink deeper into a state of complete calm, your mind will begin to as well, mirroring your body. Simply allow this relaxation to wash over you.

Now your body has started to relax, your muscles doing so too, your eyelids are becoming heavier and only more hard to keep opening. Now, I will begin to count down from 5 to 1. Feel your eyelids become heavier and heavier with each number I count. When I reach 1, your eyes will feel too heavy to open once more…

5…

4…

3…

2…

1…

Let your eyes remain closed now, feeling your eyelids be soothed as they stay closed. Now that your eyes are shut, focus on my voice, hear in deeply from within your mind. Focus on my voice alone, allowing it to guide you into relaxation, helping you release all that negativity from within your body and mind.

Now, notice that dark space between your eyes and eyelids. Remain in this empty dark nothingness, placing your consciousness right here. Though in complete darkness, you are completely safe. Here, there is nothing other than your mind and the wonderful sensations of deep relaxation, so you are completely protected and safe.

No stresses or worries from the outside world can intrude on your mental tranquility.

So as long as you are here, there is nothing that can disrupt your inner peace. Notice how deeply relaxed you feel, recognizing how refreshed your body feels and how calm and at peace your being is.

Now take this moment to visualize all the stress you feel, and how heavily this stress is weighing on your body and mind. Stress uses so much of your energy tiring the body as well as the mind. It makes the perfect environment for negative emotions to thrive, bringing pain and discomfort and even disease.

So, let us give substance to this stress and the things it brings to only hold you back. Let's imagine these stresses are large, heavy, spikey chains that are shackled to your ankles. As you try to move forward to your life goals, these shackle hold you back. With every step you take you feel pain as these shackle bite into you, weighing you down. Making your life goals seem completely impossible.

Each link in these chains represents all the negativity you take with you in life, it may be a bad relationship, or simply anything. These are the stresses that you have not yet let go of, hindering your progress. Although you may feel completely trapped, you do not have to go through your life bound like this forever.

You remain in complete control, you already have the key, the ability to free yourself from these shackles, from anything that keeps you moving forward.

Now you are going to take this opportunity to free yourself. You sit down, and begin to work on the shackles you find yourself stuck in. You see you are trapped in 5 large, sharp metal links.

The first link is your expectations. Maybe you are trying to live by someone else's expectations of you. This could be your parents expecting you to pursue certain jobs such as becoming a doctor, a lawyer, or a CEO of a company. This may be as they don't understand what you are truly capable of, so imagine a life for you that THEY think would suit you best.

Deep down inside, you know what life you want to live or at least what you don't. You may already live the life others have envisioned for you. Maybe you carried on the family business although you always dreamed of creating your own. Maybe you work as a doctor or lawyer but your true interests lie in art or entertainment.

Whatever it is, remember that this life is yours alone. Don't allow anyone else to shape it however they want, as if they own your life too. For only you know how to live your life to its fullest. Maybe now it is finally time to let go of these false expectations, and in their place set out to carve the life you have always dreamt of.

Now, take a deep breath, as you do feel that link in your shackle evaporate, melting away into the air around you. Notice how much lighter you feel now, and yet there is still more you are holding back.

Next, we will move on to the next link in the chain, this time this link represents the stress and worry from your school or work. Lots of your time is spent either at your school or work and therefore the cause of lots of stress. Right now, at this very moment this stress doesn't serve you and provides you with nothing but negativity, so let go.

Just let it go... All the worries and stress of your job or school just float away from deep within and simply disappears. Feel as you become lighter and more free, no longer weighed down by these stresses as you let go, releasing all stress.

Now, moving on to the next shackle, this time it representing any stresses brought on by money. Money can form such a huge burden, causing lots of stress. This may be the worry about making enough, being able to pay bills, will you ever have enough to live freely? Etc.

As you take this stress and worry, force it to vacate you immediately. Realize that money is just an illusion, that this is no longer something you need to worry over once more.

Trust that you will have all you ever need, that it will come to you effortlessly and simply as you need. Understand that the less you worry over money, the less of a hold it can have over your life.

You let go, along with all your worries over money. Simply let it go...

Feel as you become so much lighter now. Notice how you feel improved and refreshed as less stress weighs your body down. Although you feel great, it is not time to stop here, but to move on to the next shackle link. This time it represents the stresses brought on by all your relationships.

Stresses may be brought on by unhealthy ones or even a lack of relationships. Right now, use this safe space to completely let go of the stress that comes with these relationships. There is no need to worry about your relationships just enjoy the sensation of releasing yourself from this burden.

Just let go completely.

Finally, there is only one shackle link that holds you back. You may feel so much lighter now, but there is still no need for this to hold you back as well.

This last link represents your ego and the mind itself. Your ego and mind are truly responsible for most of the stresses and worries in your life. Your mind forms these self-sabotaging thoughts on what others think of you.

Your mind is what fills you with self-doubt, fear, vanity and so much more, but now we will no longer give it this power over you. Completely let go of thought. Letting go of all this negativity, come to realize there is no more shackle left holding you down.

Now, feel yourself completely weightless, as if you could gracefully float around free as there is no worry holding you back.

Take this time to enjoy the wonderful feeling of freedom, relaxation and weightlessness that resonates within your entire being right now. There is not a single ounce of stress left within you. There is no more worry cowering within.

Now, we are coming to the conclusion of today's meditation session. Feel free to remain here as long as you like, simply enjoying your feelings of complete freedom and relaxation. Once you are ready to return to the outside world and the day it brings, simply take a deep breath and slowly open your eyes. Enjoy your day, starting with nothing weighing you down. Thank you and see you again tomorrow.

Daily Meditation 27 (30mns)

Hello and welcome to day 27 of your wonderful 30-day meditation challenge. To begin, just get comfortable. Place your arms and legs wherever you wish, either sitting or lying down. Prioritize your comfort when getting into position now, after all, this is essential for a productive meditation session.

To begin, preparing your body for this anxiety relaxation, if you haven't done so already, close your eyes. Now, take a deep breath in using your stomach. Let the air fill your lungs completely. Exhale, emptying your lungs. Take another deep breath, in through your nose, then out through your mouth once more.

Breathe in…

And out…

In…

Out…

Keep your breathing slow and steady, completely filling and emptying your lungs with each breath. Allow your deep breathing to completely calm and relax you. Providing your body with refreshing oxygen, calming every cell.

Simply remain right here, right now in this present moment. This time is simply for you, to enjoy and relax. There is nowhere else you need to be. Simply enjoy this moment.

The focus for today's meditation is addressing any of your anxieties. You may have been through lots. You deserve and require this time, just for you, so you can function at your best. This time, will provide you with relaxation, helping you stay calm and healthy. See this as a productive time for your health, caring for yourself mentally. This is a gift to yourself, caring for all of your needs with this meditation.

Maintain the deep, steady rhythm of your breath, whilst shifting your attention to your body. Become aware of all the sensations in your body and how it feels physically. For now, you do not have to do anything, simply observe how your body feels right now.

Whatever it is you feel right now, recognize that it is okay. Don't become concerned with any physical sensations, they may be present as signs of built up stress. Simply use this time to act as an observer.

Right now, let us look for any signs of stress and tension, by performing a simple body scan. Simply look for any signs of stress, without trying to do anything with this information just yet. Starting from the top of the head, slowly working your way down scan your body.

Focusing first on your forehead. Observe how your head rests now, how its supported by your neck or whatever's beneath it. Now, move your attention down to your eyes, nose, cheeks, chin then shoulders. Notice how each area feels, how it's being held or is it resting in its natural position.

Keep scanning through your body. Focus on each little feeling, on each and every area. Gradually work your focus down to the lower parts of your body. How does your chest feel? Is it breathing freely? Note any areas of tension.

Continue you to move down your body, now to the centre of your body. As you reach the level of your stomach, note how this part feels. Simply observe your physical state move down, shifting your focus lower and lower.

As you reach the level of your hips, maintain your focus on your physical state. How does this part of your body feel? Notice any tensions, but simply leave them as they are for now. Once more, move your focus downward.

Now at the level of your knees, how does this level feel? Note any tension. Continue scanning through your body... All the way down to the tip of the toes. Now you have scanned through your entire body, take this moment to work your way back up through your body once more. How does your body feel as a whole? Where in your body is holding the most tension?

Focus on this one area of tension now. Imagine the muscles in this area loosen, lengthening, and releasing all their tension. Feel the cool air from your inhales target this area, relaxing it, releasing all the tension, bit by bit with every exhale.

Feel as the tension throughout your body begins to soften. Allow your muscles to relax, loosen, and stretch as if they are being soothed by the air as you breathe.

Note where in your body feels the most relaxed. How does it feel? Focus firstly on this area, giving these feelings of relaxation substance. Give it a colour, feel how it feels. Now, feel this sensation grow throughout your being, feel your body becoming illuminated by this colour, tingling as it slowly spreads through you.

Enjoy as this feeling of relaxation spreads through your body, making you feel at ease and in complete peace, as you continue with this meditation.

Now, envision the air you breathe carries an energy, allowing you to completely relax. With every inhale, the air that fills you fills you with relaxation too, with every exhale the air carries away all your stress and tensions. Now, your breathing acts as an efficient relaxation system. Relaxation takes over with each and every breath. Your body expels tension with your exhale, straight out through your mouth.

Breathe in…

And breathe out…

Continue to breathe deeply in this way for the next few moments, allowing yourself to sink deeper into a state of complete relaxation.

(Pause 1mn)

Soon, all the tensions you hold onto will be so small you can barely feel they are there. Any your body holds onto now, imagine simply breathing it all out. Your breath alone has the power to eliminate those tensions. Feel yourself calm and relaxed. Your system refreshed and clear… Breathing in relaxation and breathing out any stresses.

Take a deep breath in… and relax…

Now, breathe out… Relax…

Maintain the slow and steady rhythm of your breath. Feel as your body sinks deeper into relaxation with each breath. As you continue with this meditation, take this next moment to scan through your body once more. Notice how it feels now.

Start from the top of your head… Moving down… to the tips of your toes…

(Pause 2mns)

Now, using your imagination, envision your body is something that can change state such as chocolate. Right now, your body is a hard, solid piece of chocolate. Imagine now, a feeling of soothing warmth, spreading through you, straight from your heart. This familiar warmth begins to soften your body.

Soon, your hands and feet will feel so soft, as if they are liquid. As this gentle warmth spreads throughout your body, radiating from your heart down to the tips of your toes and the very top of your head. Let this pleasant feeling relax you further.

Relax as this warmth spreads, melting your body. Feel as this warmth reaches your hands and feet, notice it completely softens and relaxes them.

Now, your body is soft, and smooth like melted chocolate, extremely impressionable by any positive energy. Take this next moment to enjoy this relaxing sensation.

(Pause 1mn)

Now, shift you focus to your thoughts. As you enjoy this relaxation observe your calming thoughts. Obtaining complete peace and relaxation can be done simply by focusing on a single word. So, as you meditate, focus on the word "relax", mentally say it with each inhale and exhale.

Breathe in, "relax"

Breathe out, "relax"

Keep to the slow and steady pace of your breathing, repeating "relax" in your mind each time you inhale and again when you exhale. Continue to do this. It is okay if mind starts to wander, although gently guide your focus back to the word "relax". Keep repeating this word as you continue to breathe.

Focus... Relax...

Keep repeating this word…

As you find yourself drifting into a state of relaxation, notice how you are completely calm. Now simply focus on nothing at all. Let your mind drift if it needs. Just be in this moment.

Just… Rest… Relax… Enjoy this pleasant state you find yourself in. Allow yourself to continue relaxing a while longer… Enjoy this pleasant, calmness… Enjoy this time, time simply for yourself … You deserve this rest… Continue meditating…

Remember that you have created this safe space just for you. That it is always here ready for your return if ever you need. When you leave this place, the feeling of calm will remain with you wherever you go…

In your daily life, even as you encounter stress, this feeling of calm confidence is still with you. If ever you start to feel anxious, this place of peace can be easily accessed just by thinking of it. Using this to your knowledge you may find that the anxiety goes away in an instant… Trust in your knowledge of this peaceful place, using it in stressful situations or times of anxiousness, and find your confidence and composure display only calmness as you face these stresses.

Take a deep breath in…

Hold, feeling Relaxed…

And breathe out… Emptying your lungs…

Keep breathing calmly and smoothly. Maintaining this cycle of breathing, taking in relaxation whilst pushing out any tension. Imagine that with each breath you become more resilient against the harsh realities of life, better equipped to deal with any stresses that come your way.

Now we come to the end of today's session. So whenever you're ready, take a deep breath and slowly open your eyes. Smile, stretch and have a good day. Thank you and see you again tomorrow.

Daily Meditation 28 (40mns)

Hello and welcome to day 28 of your 30-day meditation. The end of this challenge is close, near in sight. The deep satisfaction of completing this challenge is yet a step nearer. After completion you would have developed a love for meditation, with an enjoyment for the small almost insignificant things, enriching your outlook on life and its beauties.

So, it is time to prepare yourself for today's session, get yourself into whatever position you find comfortable. This can be however you like, but your comfort remains of importance to maximize the productiveness of this session.

Once you are comfortably settled, take a deep breath and we will begin with a simple breathing exercise. Today, we will do something a little different, so don't feel as if you have to close your eyes just yet. Allow your mind and eyes to wander or simply focus on any area in your immediate surroundings.

Now, go ahead and take a deep breath, feel as the air fills your lungs. With you exhale, feel relief as your body begins to release any build ups of stress.

Again, take another deep breath in, and as you do close your eyes. Then, hold your breath at the top for a few seconds. When you exhale, open your eyes again. Continue this pattern of breathing, and opening and closing your eyes or until you feel your eyelids become too heavy.

(Pause 1mn)

At this point, your eyes should have begun to feel very heavy. So, now go right ahead and close your eyes. While your vision fades to darkness, shift your focus to your breathing.

Give yourself complete permission to relax. Take this meditation and this form of self-care, allowing your entire being to receive this love and care. Relish in meditations ability to solve many problems even modern medicine cannot.

Meditation improves your sleep, helping your performance in your day. It can act as a cure for anxiety and worry, relieving your body and mind from stress, that you can't even escape from in sleep. If you feel stressed and don't unwind before you sleep, you will wake pent up the next morning.

So, we will work on relieving the body and mind from these stresses and worries. Now, quiet your mind, turn your attention inward, as we focus on relaxing the body... Letting your muscles relax.

Now, take a moment, and using your imagination envision what relaxation feels like. It may be a particular tingly sensation, you find pleasurable. It may feel warm, cool, heavy, or light. The feeling of relaxation differs from person to person. So regardless of however it feels to you, it is a peaceful, pleasant feeling. It simply feels comfortable and something you will never not appreciate.

Now, to truly feel the effects of relaxation, we will start to check in with your body. We want the muscles to completely relax, so note any areas of tension that prevent this. Now, notice as your chest rise and falls gently with each breath, and how this brings even more feelings of relaxation.

As your chest lowers from your exhale, imagine that all tension leaves your body, carried by the air of your breath. As you continue to breathe, feel yourself sink deeper into a deep state of relaxation.

Take this moment to notice how relaxed you are. As you breathe, feel any leftover tensions be carried away by your breath. Allowing yourself to sink deeper into relaxation. Relaxing in this way is essential, refreshing and rejuvenating your body so you feel energetic after this session.

Simply relax, and let go. You are, as always, in total control. You can leave whenever you wish. You can bring your consciousness back with your body, moving forward with your day at any point. When you feel it is time to leave, you will feel totally alert and completely refreshed. Right now, simply let yourself drift pleasantly.

Relax…

Right now, just being present in this meditation, you are working towards the relief from various problems such as insomnia, which can be caused by your minds mental worry. It also helps to relieve anxiety, as this is the typical response to fear, yet you find yourself in no harm.

All your worries and stresses you hold onto, make your life harder as they slow you down, attempting to hinder you from progressing in life. Think of these things as a web that holds you from doing your best. You may feel trapped in this web, but through meditation and relaxation, you can free yourself.

With a refreshed and energized body and mind, you can truly perform at your best. This way, at the end of your day you will feel accomplished and ready for a completely restful sleep, and then waking up the next day feeling even better.

Through meditation alone, you can gain so much. So far through this 30-day challenge, you may have begun to see the magical effects meditation can have on you. You may have lived for so long plagued with a negative state of mind, seemingly unescapable.

So, right now call upon memories that bring you peace or happy stories of your day ahead. Most importantly think of anything that brings you peaceful, pleasant bodily sensations, relaxing your muscles and mind completely.

Relaxation is necessary for your growth. Just as your mind may use memory and imagination for easier worrying, we will use them for easy relaxation. Right now using minimal effort, and simply using the power of your imagination, you can relax.

Take this moment, using this opportunity to give your mind a break from worry, and deal with stress. Allow your mind this time, to break away, vacating away from your stresses and worries, preparing you for your day.

You are in control. You can deal with any negativities that find themselves in your life. You can attain inner peace, simply using the power of your imagination. So, let us use this power right now, to focus your mind… Giving it a mental break from all worldly worries.

Whenever you find thoughts of worry intruding your inner peace, recall this feeling of tranquility you have within you right now. As you do this, tell yourself to breathe, focusing on your chest as it gently rises and falls, allowing it to soothe and calm you, allowing no space left for these worries.

Using the beautiful tool of imagination, we will focus the mind elsewhere. So now, externalize all negativity from inside you. Think of it as a dark, deep, and damp cave. An unpleasant place, so clammy it feels as if you can't breathe. You may find yourself here right now, or trapped halfway out towards where you want to be: Peace. Where is this peace located?

The peace you look for is the opposite of this dark, overwhelming cave of negativity. It may be bright and open, on a beach, or a vast meadow of wild flowers. When you remain here in this cave, you feel stressed and under strain.

So, give yourself permission to move on out of this cave, towards the light, to your magical place of peace that will provide you the relaxation you need to refresh your body and mind. With each inhale, you take another step forward towards the light. As you exhale, let go of all the negativity that has a hold over you, leaving it behind cowering in the darkness of this cave.

(Pause 1mn)

Now, you have arrived at your magical place. You may have been here before or be a completely fictitious location. This place could be anywhere, all that matters is that you feel safe and relaxed. Don't use lots of your mind energy to conjure up such a place, simply allow your mind to bring it to you. After all, your mind knows exactly what you need to relax.

Once you find yourself in your special place of peace, take a moment and just explore. Allow your senses to be filled with all it has to offer. Hear its gentle song. Feel your skin absorb its gentle light as well as its heat or coldness. Taste this place on your tongue. Smell its sweet scent right in your nose. Simply take the next couple minutes to explore its wonders right now.

(Pause 2mn)

Let the energy of this place bring tranquility to your entire being. Simply let go, welcoming this positivity as it seeps into your every cell. Let relaxation come to you. As you breathe, feel the relaxing energy in the air enter. With your exhale let go of all your worries.

Here, you are safe. You are in complete control, so nothing can harm you here as everything is yours. No worldly worries are welcome, so they simply can't reach you here. This place is just for you. For you to rejuvenate and refresh on its soothing energy.

Now, you may find your mind begins to wander at this point in the session. If so, simply take a deep breath and guide your focus back to your breath. Right now this time is for relaxation alone, so there is no space for worry.

So, repeat my words into reality saying after me: "I am safe. I am perfect just the way I am. I accept and receive all positivity in life. I have worries and troubling thoughts, but my body and mind come first. I choose to care for myself and relax, so I can achieve my best in all aspects of life."

Let relaxation and inner peace occur naturally. Allow your unconscious to take over. Let its soft and gentle whispers, carry you far away from all that negativity, and towards complete positivity, that magical place of light, the place where you long to be.

Let your minds soothing words work their magic. Imagine these gentle murmurs coming to life and transporting you directly to your peaceful place. Better yet, imagine them gently floating you towards this sense of deep relaxation.

Understand your worrying thoughts try their hardest to keep you from this sense of peace. Telling your mind to stay with them and their negativity, as they cause tight sensations all over your body while you become entrapped in their cycle of negativity. As you exhale, allow them to be swept away, and whatever is left is erased by your kind words you whisper to yourself.

Again, repeat after me: "I love myself. I choose to give myself this time and space to relax and energize, as I know that I am not worthy of all the problems in my life. I chose to give myself this invaluable, beautiful gift of relaxation. I am at peace. I am refreshed. I am perfect."

Now, your worries are gone, so go right ahead and take another deep breath. With this new found space, once being taken over by negativity, allow yourself to bring in yet more of the air's refreshing, soothing energy. Feel as your body and mind sinks deeper into relaxation. Take this moment and simply have gratitude for yourself, for you have given yourself this opportunity to rejuvenate, repair and refresh your body and mind.

Take this energy and feelings of relaxation with you to the outside world. Now you have accessed this place once, you have already created a new pathway, a connection, linking you to this magical place. So, whenever you next need, you will be able to find your way back here to rejuvenate and repair yourself.

Simply through meditation you can find your way back here. As meditation opens pathways for you, including access to this magical place of peace. Whenever you find yourself in a stressful situation and feel yourself becoming overwhelmed you can return to this place.

Now we come to the conclusion of today's meditation, you may choose to remain in this place of peace for a while longer. Whenever you are ready to return to your day, simply take a deep breath and slowly open your eyes. Have a great day. Thank you and see you again tomorrow.

Daily Meditation 29 (40mns)

Hello and welcome to day 29 of your 30-day meditation challenge. To begin, get yourself into a comfortable position, whatever you have found works best for you. Then, take a deep breath, in through your nose, and slowly back out your mouth. Close your eyes, and as your vision fades into darkness, shift your focus to your breath.

Now, after each inhale and exhale, simply hold while we count up to four, allowing your body as much time as necessary to absorb all the oxygen it needs to unwind and relax.

Breathe in... 1, 2, 3, and 4...

And out... 1, 2, 3, and 4...

Now, repeat this two more times...

In... 1, 2, 3, and 4...

And out... 1, 2, 3, and 4...

One more...

In... 1, 2, 3, and 4...

And out... 1, 2, 3, and 4...

Perfect. Now, let us work on relaxing the body, so let us check in with it now, starting with a simple body scan exercise. So simply looking for any signs of stress, shift your focus to the top of your head, and let us begin to scan each area of the body.

Starting from your forehead, focus your mind here, breathing intently to soothe the muscles in that area. Slowly move your focus down to your brows, nose, cheeks, lips, chin, neck... Slowly down to your shoulders, arms, fingers, chest, stomach... To your back... hips... legs... and toes...

Whenever you come across any areas of tension, simply breath intently into them, allowing the power of your breath to soothe that area, relaxing them. Allow the air you breathe, to carry away all the stress and tension from within you. Carrying it out as you exhale.

So, spend the next few moments with your body now, as you relax your every muscle.

(Pause 2mns)

Now, we will take this next moment to check in with your mind. What kind of state is it in today? Does it look as if it will be a day full of negative, obsessive thoughts? Or does it look as if today it will be quiet and calm? Whatever your minds current outlook of today, right now we will ensure your state of mind and body are protected from this negativity.

For now, simply focus on your breathing. Observe how the powerful air flows in and back out of your body. Notice how your chest gently rises and falls with every breath. Feel how the air fills and inflates your lungs. Notice how the air flows through you. Does it travel with ease? Or is this journey interrupted by your shallow breaths? Or maybe even feelings of constrain. Either way simply remain with your breath for the next minute or so, allowing the air it brings to enter, soothing your body and mind.

(Pause 1mn)

Now, to take you further into relaxation, imagine you are standing in a vast field of wildflowers. The sun shines happily above you. You see the sky is a beautiful blue, dotted with a few white, fluffy clouds that float harmoniously across the sky. As you take a deep breath, you feel a gentle breeze ruffle through your hair. Enjoy the warmth of the sun, allowing it to soothe all the muscles in your body, relaxing you further.

Focus on this warmth now, as the sun overhead showers you with its radiant light, seemingly casting you into a spotlight. Feel as if the sun has chosen you alone to focus its healing energy on, soothing and relaxing every cell in your body. Take another deep breath and simply let go. Let go, welcoming this lights potent energy, allowing your body to soak up every last drop of its relaxing energy.

Now, focus that warm, calming sensation on your feet. Feel them become heavy with relaxation. Allow this warmth and weight spread up through to your calf and then your knees.

Enjoy the sensation this sunlight brings, as it soothes your thighs and then continues to work its way up to your hips. Now your entire legs are heavy, comfortable and relaxed as this magical sunlight displaces all pain and tension from within.

Now, allow this warmth to envelop your pelvis, lower back, and then your abdomen. Feel as your entire lower body becomes heavy, warm, and soothed as this energy relaxes your muscles, releasing any build ups of tension that may have gathered.

Feel this light spread through you further, reaching up to your chest with its comforting warmth. With each and every breath, feel yourself becoming yet more relaxed.

So, give yourself permission to absorb all of this suns warm, refreshing energy. Allow this warmth flow through your arms to your hands now. Feel as this soothing sensation washes through to your fingertips, allowing them to return to their natural gentle curl. Notice now how your entire arms have absorbed this energy, as they feel heavier and completely relaxed.

Now, feel this pleasant sensation as it proceeds up to your shoulders and then spreading into your neck. Feel your neck as the sunlight's energy soothes the muscles here, loosening and relaxing them. Visualize this energy as it expands through your being, up to your jaw, mouth, cheeks, eyes, and forehead.

Take this moment to truly enjoy your entire being becoming enveloped by this beautiful, pleasant and relaxing sensation, right from the very top of your head down to the tips of your toes.

Now, notice how your entire body is brimming with the suns warm energy. Every area of your being, every muscle, every tissue, and even your every molecule has been touched by this energy, and now feels heavy and relaxed. Notice your breathing, its rhythm slow, deep and easy. You are completely at peace. You are calm now, as you drift further from stress and deeper into a state of relaxation and peace.

Simply appreciate right now. Take a moment and just give yourself thanks, for you have gifted yourself this relaxation session. Simply by using this time and space, you are giving your body and mind the opportunity to heal, to soothe, and to rejuvenate. This gift is invaluable, nothing money can simply buy. Just by using this time from your busy day to meditate, it gives your body the relief it needs, so that you can perform your best. Right now, you have chosen to put the care of your body and mind first.

So smile, and have gratitude for this act of self-love. You recognize and understand that you deserve the best of life, and this is the first step towards a better life. Smile as you have given yourself this gift, rewarding yourself for your hard work, with refreshing energy and relaxation that meditation brings. Smile because you have chosen to nourish your mind with complete peace, just like you nourish your body with food.

So now, simply spend the next couple of minutes with your breath. Anchor yourself to this present moment with your gentle inhales and exhales. Your mind may wander, but if so, take a deep breath and guide your focus back to your breath

(Pause 2mns)

Now, using the power of your imagination, picture yourself stood on a beach. This beach is small, secluded yet beautiful. Feel the gentle breeze from the sea, ruffle through your clothes whilst a gentle calmness washes over you. Take a deep breath in, smelling the salty air as it passes through your nostrils.

This day is wonderfully warm and serene. You feel the warm, white sand massage your feet. As you look down and wiggle your toes, the ivory sand soothingly slinks through your toes.

Simply appreciate this beautiful place you find yourself in, as you slip deeper into relaxation while you enjoy this simple, quiet moment. Listen as the waves gently wash over the shore, as they break into the glistening sand, and flow back out to sea once more.

Become one with this place, synchronize your breathing with the waves. As the waves crash in, take a breath in. As they flow back out to sea, exhale. With every wave that washes up to shore, feel yourself becoming more and more relaxed. More and more calm. And more and more at peace.

Now, any discomforts and stresses that remain within you, that you may have been experiencing recently, allow them to melt out of your feet and be carried away with each wave, into the vast ocean. While you watch any of your stresses float away, you see the clearness of the water. Below you see the sand swirling gently as each wave comes and goes.

As you look up, towards the horizon, watch as the small sailboats continue their own journey, gliding with ease along the surface of the water. Look up further and see the clouds float casually overhead, forming shapes as they drift across the sky.

Now, take in a deep breath.

Breathe in...

And out...

Feel as you become warmer, cozier, more relaxed, and calm. Feel the suns soothing warmth start to touch the very top of your head, gradually flowing down to your toes, allowing your every cell to relax completely.

You place a blanket down on the warm sand, and begin to bathe in the sun's relaxing warming energy. You feel the warmth of the sun gently kiss your skin, and a sense of relaxation washes over your entire body. You close your eyes, inviting the sun's warmth to settle on your further.

The day is beautiful. As you lay there, listening to the calming crashes of the waves, this sound soothes you. Each wave washes away any tensions and worries you find yourself holding onto, carrying them straight out to the sea.

Now, take this moment to scan through your body once more, notice any areas of discomfort. Using your mind's eyes, give this sense of discomfort a colour. Think of what colour best suits the discomfort. It could be red, black, whatever you think is best. Then, give this discomfort a shape. Again, envision what shape truly illustrates it. Then, give it a texture, maybe rough? Whatever you wish. As you focus on the color, shape, and texture, take a deep breath, and begin to notice the color change.

Its colour may change shade, becoming paler or even change colour completely. However this colour decides to change, recognize that this signifies any discomfort slowly dissipating. Notice also, how the shape changes too, wearing down or disintegrating completely.

Continue to focus on that discomfort, notice how it slowly disappears and you are becoming more and more relaxed.

Now, using the power of your imagination, start to see a very restful, special place. Sense all this special place has to offer. Now, let us count from 1 to 5, and as you do so, feel yourself become completely immersed in this comfortable and peaceful sanctuary.

1... just relax into your safe place...

2...Enjoy it here...

3... You may have been here before...

4... It may be a new place you have created here in the moment...

And 5...

Now, you have been welcomed and have become perfectly settled into your sanctuary, your safe haven. This place is always awaiting your arrival. Whenever you are feeling overwhelmed or stressed, and in need of a break from everyday worries, you can always return here to this sense of deep comfort and relaxation.

You are in complete control. Only you have the key to access this place, through your meditation. Even just thinking of this special place brings you relaxation. You control this place and what can enter this wonderful safe haven.

Now we come to the end of this session, but feel free to remain in your place of relaxation. Once you are ready to return to your busy day, simply take a deep breath and slowly open your eyes. Smile in gratitude, as you have completed another session in our 30-day meditation challenge. Thank you and see you again tomorrow.

Daily Meditation 30 (40mns)

Hello and welcome to the final day of your 30-day meditation challenge. After the completion of today's session, you will have completed this challenge as well as a healthy habit for meditation.

So, let us begin. Get comfortable, in whatever position you wish. Have your arms and legs wherever feels natural, just a long as you are comfortable. Remember, comfort is key, maximizing the productiveness of this meditation session.

So let's begin this session, if you haven't already take a deep breath in… And out… And slowly close your eyes. While your vision fades into darkness, shift your focus to your breath.

Now, using your stomach, take another deep breath in, allow the cool air to enter expanding your lungs fully, then breathe out, emptying them completely. Take another deep breath, in through your nose. Allow the air to leave again out through your mouth.

Breathe in…

And out…

In…

Out…

Continue this slow and steady rhythm of breathing. Allowing your lungs to completely fill and then emptying again with every inhale and exhale.

Your deep breathing has the powerful ability to relax and calm you. It allows your body to receive all the oxygen it needs, so it can begin to refresh and relax itself.

Remain completely in this present moment. Right now all that concerns you is right here, nothing can disturb you from this relaxation. Simply enjoy this time just for yourself. Enjoy how you feel right here. Over the course of these 30 days, you may have experienced lots of important life events outside of this session. Some of which may have brought you lots of stress, demanding lots of your time, energy and most importantly strong mental and physical health.

For this reason, you deserve this moment simply for yourself. Although this time may be brief, this session will bring you all the calm and relaxing energy you need for your mind, body and spirit to feel refreshed and rejuvenated. Trust that this time is not being wastefully spent. As you understand the productive effect on your health this session has on you. This time, spent through meditation, is vital in ensuring all aspects of your health are cared for.

So now, it is time to check in with the mind and its current state. At any point in this session, you may find your mind start to wander, which is only natural. Even those most practiced in meditation cannot maintain focus at all times. When you find your mind does so, simply check in with each thought, uncovering why it is there. This may simply be a result of the mind's boredom. Sometimes these thoughts bring up emotions of worry and anxiety, which are more difficult to uncover the true meaning behind.

Whatever the thoughts are, they may be trying to tell you something, so simply remain with them for a few seconds, and no longer. Simply acknowledge their existence and why they may be present, before moving on.

Now for the next couple minutes, simply remain with your thoughts, using this time to let your mind wander. Study each passing thought briefly, before moving onto the next. Remind yourself to not get caught in any emotions they may bring. Simply act as an observer to your own thoughts.

(Pause 2mns)

Now, continue to breathe deeply and steadily, shift your focus to your body. The next step in this session is checking in with the body, noticing how it feels, and making sure it is fully relaxed. So, check in with your physical body, noticing how it feels right now. For now, all you need to do is observe any areas that are in pain or holding any stress or tension. Just become aware of how you feel in general.

Maintain this slow and steady rhythm of your breath. Notice any physical sensations you feel in your body right now. You don't have to do anything right now, just spend this time with your body.

Removing all judgement, observe how your body feels. Whatever you feel right now, recognize these feelings are valid and exist just for now. While you check in with your physical body, some areas may feel very relaxed and calm. Others may not, showing you signs of built-up stress. For now, just observe any bodily sensations such as a gentle tingling, or feelings of heavy calmness. For now, just note any signs of stress and tension that you may have.

Now, we will scan the entire body in great depth, and begin to relax any areas that are stubbornly holding onto tension. So, start from the top of your head and move down through your body slowly. Notice your heads position, does it feel supported by your neck or the pillow beneath you? Take this moment to make sure it does.

Then, begin to move your attention slowly down to your forehead. Are you tensing your forehead? If so, simply take a deep breath and allow this area to relax. Now, move down to your brows, again, are your brows are furrowed and tensed, if so, take a deep breath and let them loosen and relax.

Now, pay attention to your eyelids. Are they resting naturally, or do you find yourself squeezing them tightly shut? Take a deep breath now, and let go, allow your eyelids to relax, resting neutrally where is natural.

Continue to work through every part of your face, relaxing them as you go. Then gradually work down to your neck, then your shoulders. Do you find yourself holding them in a certain position? Take a deep breath and let go, allowing your arms to hang gently and weightlessly from your shoulders.

Continue to work through your body slowly, scanning for any areas that feel tense or in pain. Slowly move your attention down, down through your body, towards your toes. Now, reaching your chest level, how does this area feel? Noticing any areas holding tension.

As you move your attention to the centre of your body, at around stomach level, observe how this area is feeling. Keep your focus on the observation of your physical state. Continue to scan your body, whilst shifting your focus lower and lower.

Now as you reach the level of your hips. How do you feel here? Continue observing whilst moving your attention downwards. As you come across any signs of tension, don't try to change anything.

Now, while you reach the level of your knees, notice how your holding them, and any sensations you feel in this area. Continue to scan through your body now, until finally, you reach the very tips of your toes.

Now, take this moment to scan through your body as a whole, once again. Overall how does your body feel today? Where do you find holds the most tension? Wherever this may be, shift your focus to the area intently. Use your imagination to visualize this area's tension. Give it a shape and colour. Perhaps is looks like a sharp, red spike, or maybe an oozing yellow blob of liquid.

Whatever you picture the form of this tension, by giving it substance, it allows us to break it down much more easily. So once you have given it a form, take a deep breath filled with intention. Feel the fresh air infiltrate whatever form your tension lies in, soothing the area. With each breath, feel as that blob or sharp spike of pain slowly disintegrates. Continue to breathe deeply and intently, and feel as all your bodily pains are soothed and carried away. Continue to do this for the next few moments, so every last ounce of your body is pain-free and relaxed.

(Pause 3mns)

Now, shift your focus to where in your body feels the most relaxed. Sense this area with your mind, observing all it feels. Again, using your mind's eyes, give it substance. Perhaps it is in the form of glistening, melted gold just gently warm. With each breath you take, feel as it travels smoothly through your bloodstream, spreading slowly throughout your body.

As you breathe, feel this healing, gold liquid soak through every fiber of your being, every tissue, every cell, all coated abundantly in this healing energy. While you continue to breathe, enjoy the feeling of this magical, healing aura spreading throughout your entire being.

Now, imagine that the air you inhale has the exact properties of energy your body needs to rejuvenate and refresh. Imagine the air as it enters as relaxation, whilst the air you breathe out is the exhaustion, stress, and tension that creeps into your body. As you inhale and exhale, feel the gentle stillness of this relaxation. Simply remain here with your body for the next moment as it introduces you to complete peace, free from all your worldly worries.

(Pause 1mns)

Enjoy the gentle, relaxation that enters with each and every breath. Whilst continuing to expel all leftover tension in your body, out through your mouth as you exhale. Continue to accept relaxation in through the nose, whilst releasing tension out through your mouth. Continue this pattern of breathing, allowing your body to fully relax. Notice how your most relaxed area is now growing bigger as you breathe in, and any areas of tension diminish as you breathe out.

So, breathe in...

And breathe out...

Each breath you take only adds to the sensation of relaxation, providing your body and mind yet more energy for its rejuvenation. With each and every exhale, feel all stress and tension within shrink, until no more. Maintain your slow and steady rhythm of breath, and allow yourself to sink deeper into relaxation.

Now, at this point, all your body should feel very relaxed, calm, and pain-free. You now feel relaxed, at peace even. Your entire system is refreshed and optimized.

Take a deep breath in... Relax further...

Now, breathe out... Just relax...

Continue to breathe in this way. Maintain your slow and steady pace and feel your body sink deeper into relaxation, with each breath you take. While you continue this meditation, scan through your body once more. Notice how your body feels now.

So starting from the top of your head... Slowly moving downwards until you reach the very tips of your toes. Every single cell, every molecule of your being is relaxed and comfortable. Relish in the lack of tension, and only relaxation, and comfort.

(Pause 1mn)

At this point, your focus remains on meditation alone, nothing else. You may realize things you need to take care of, ready for your busy day ahead. Whatever you may need to do, right now is not the time to stress. Right now, this moment is simply for you. You time for relaxation and rejuvenation. Just remain here, enjoy the stillness, the calm of right now.

Now, let us bring our focus back to our thoughts once more. You may have noticed that your thoughts are much calmer and less intrusive, than they were 30 days ago, when we began this challenge. Enjoy the company of your calm thoughts while you simply relax.

Now at this point, you will have developed the ability to achieve relaxation as and when desired. All possible by combining all of meditations powerful, healing, energy, simply by focusing your attention to the word "relax".

So, let us use this moment to focus on this word right now. Mentally repeat it to yourself every time you breathe in and out. Breathe in… Relax… Breathe out… Relax…

Continue to breathe, saying this word to yourself in this way, for the next moment. Saying "Relax" with every inhale and exhale.

(Pause 1mn)

You may find your mind begins to wander once more. This is okay. Simply use the word "Relax" as a tool to return your focus to this meditation. Continue to repeat this to yourself whilst you meditate, allowing relaxation to seep in.

Focus… And relax… Continue to repeat the word "Relax" to yourself.

Now, notice how completely relaxed and calm you are. You are filled with energy yet not frantic. You feel calm yet not sleepy tired. So, shifting your focus back to your breath, and simply enjoy the last few minutes of this meditation, in your current pleasant, relaxed and refreshed state.

(Pause 1mn)

Now we come to the conclusion of this meditation. Be proud that you have made it to the last day of this 30-day meditation challenge. That you have unlocked the ability to provide yourself with true relaxation and mental tranquility. That you have taken and now know the steps to unlocking your full potential, simply by allowing yourself to retreat to your inner mind whenever you need. Congratulations!

When you wish to achieve a deeper relaxation for a restful sleep or to cope with stressful situations, you can use the power of meditation, so make sure to check out the next two sessions for improved sleep.

Whenever you are ready to return to the outside world, to your day, simply take a deep breath and slowly open your eyes. Feel refreshed, ready for your day ahead. Thank you and have a nice day.

A Walk Along The Lake - A Bedtime Story (30 Minutes)

Hello and good evening. Tonight, we will take a calming stroll along the lake. Before we begin, make sure you are in a comfortable and cozy position. Now, take a few deep breaths. Release any tension you may be holding onto, as you breathe out. Release any tension left over from your day, it is no longer needed now. Whenever you are ready, gently close your eyes. Now, our magical walk will commence.

As you look over the lake today, you notice its beauty and calming stillness. It looks just like a smooth, silk, crystal blanket. You imagine on a warm summers day, it would feel wonderful to take a dip, allowing the cool, calming blanket of water to wash over you. Making you feel more connected and one with nature and all its beauties.

The water, so still acts as a mirror, reflecting the trees warm, fiery leaves and the blue sky back to you. You take a deep breath in, appreciating the refreshing, local air. You feel energized as this cool, crisp air fills your lungs and feel release as you breathe out all your worries and stresses on your mind. You feel you need not carry these thoughts with you here, so you release them all freely and without second thought.

Now, as you begin to walk forward, you watch as a small group of ducks make their way into the water, along the embankment opposite to you. Up until now, it felt as if you were the only living thing around. Seeing them calmly go about their day, not restricted by time reminds you how full of life this lake, truly is. For these ducks, this blissful place is somewhere they are lucky enough to call home. You watch the surface of the water as the ducks swim. As they glide with ease, they create tiny ripples that move on out growing wider until they fade away once more.

You watch as the ducks swim further into the distance, until they cease to exist. Now the only way you can prove their presence here is the small rippling effect their swimming has had on the surface of the water. Just tiny, gentle ripples on the otherwise smooth, still surface.

Now, you continue to walk further down the embankment of the lake, until you reach a worn, once loved fishing boat. This boat, although it seems to have been through a lot in its life, still looks warm and inviting, tempting you to take of inside it. You imagine what joys taking this boat out onto these calm waters, would provide. To simply sit and fish for hours on end, enjoying the company of these calm waters. You wonder if there are many beautiful fish that call this lake their home. Although as you reflect on this, that may not be the point. Simply enjoying the total peace this place provides you, a place you can remain with yourself as well as the beautiful surroundings is all you need when on this boat.

This lake is so large it seems to stretch out completely into the horizon. Although you have come here for a quick walk, the lakes enormousness does not intimidate you. If you are here for hours on end, it doesn't seem to matter now. The wonderful scenery and the calmness it provides you with, are so inviting you could stay here all day. You continue to breathe in this refreshing air, simply taking in all the lake has to offer. You imagine yourself wandering about, around the entire lake, before climbing in the boat and taking it out onto the still water. As you joyfully sit in the boat, you imagine yourself drinking a flask of tea, just watching the day go by, slowly turning into night before you. As you do so, you enjoy the reflection of the water provide you a perfect screen as you watch the sun's bright ray gradually be replaced with the glistening moon and stars.

You reflect on the accepted fast paced life that most people follow. Why don't more people come to places like this? The unrelenting nature of today's life, filled with technology and work means that many people feel as if they never have an opportunity to just switch off. That it is widely accepted, never having a moment where the focus is simply on being alive. Place like this, seemingly are the solution, exactly what people need. Right here, in this place, time is no constraint. Time is slowed down, and does not bother you. You don't feel as if you should be anywhere else, or thinking of other things. Here, all you do is notice the beauty of the lake, and how it connects you with nature. Connect with the true world.

By this lake, you don't want to rush. You simply want to relish in this moment and if anything, you would like to walk a little slower while you move around the lake. Just valuably spending your time. Fully embracing this current moment of peace and closeness with that around you. This experience is not one you want to rush. You have as much time as you need, to simply breathe it all in.

Around you, there is little to no noise. Every once in a while, you can hear the gentle ripple of the water, although even this is very faint. As you walk past any patches of long grass, you can hear the occasional stick insect's song, almost greeting you as you walk by. This lake, is far enough away from civilization, that you can't hear the gentle rumble of cars on the road or people's voices. Normally, these sounds are hard to escape and distance yourself from. But here, these sounds are out of place, and simply don't belong.

Now as you continue walk along, you notice a small pub on the other side, far of in the distance but still in your vision. It looks warm and quiet, seemingly beckoning you towards it. Just outside this pub, stands benches facing out onto the lake. You think that as you pass it, you may have to stop by and have a cool drink. A welcoming chance to rest your legs before you carry on walking, down by the other side of the lake.

You wonder if many people visit this pub each day, for now it looks very quiet. Then again, you imagine this quiet atmosphere is what sells the place to many, continuing ones' sense of calming solitude, that this characteristic attracts many, like you inside. The landlords sole focus may well be, to simply provide his customers a chance to remain still, while enjoying a refreshing drink in the midday sun.

Now, you have decided that when you reach this pub, you will have a sit down. For now, you are not in any rush. There is no need to fasten your pace to get there, as right now, time has no meaning and you can take as long as you like. As you walk, you feel no sense of urgency, as you know you will reach it eventually. For now, you decide that you are going to stop at the pub once you get there, but you are not in a rush. You do not need to get there in a hurry. You know that right now time has no meaning. There is no urgency as you walk. You know you will reach the pub eventually. For now, all you have to do is keep walking peacefully along the lake simply appreciating your calm surroundings.

Every now and then, you watch as a group of small, colourful birds flying around the lake. Occasionally, some of them drop down to eat small seeds and nuts, or attempt to dig out worms from the dusty ground. A few, smoothly glide by your head, landing quite very near you. As you share this space, they have no reason to be fearful of you or your presence. You give of such a calm and relaxed aura that these birds trust you mean them no harm, that you have no issue sharing the magical sensations this lake and its surroundings provide. Similar to the stick insects, you find some of them chirp to you in greeting as you walk past. You smile back in response, while they register your good nature.

As you near the pub, you walk by another group of ducks making their way down into the clear, still waters of the lake. You take a moment and wonder if they are on the move to greet the other group that you saw earlier. They glide softly along the water's surface clinging closely to the opposite side of the lake. As they swim, they pass below a low hanging tree branch. It acts as a parasol, providing them just a few brief moments away from the suns glare before they feel its warmth once more. The slow down slightly, as they pass under the branch, savouring the cool calmness it gives them. A brief moment to cool themselves slightly. It's not that the suns warmth is uncomfortable. More that this shade is a soothing, contrasting experience, they feel should be treasured. Much like you feel with your walk along the edge of the lake right now.

Now you find yourself at the pub, you once saw as only a distant spec. You order a large drink with ice, and you take a seat on one of the benches outside. As you take a sip, you stretch out your feet in front of you. The coolness of your drink as it slides down your throat, fills your body, making you feel completely relaxed and refreshed. Enjoying this moment, you look over the lake before you and gently close your eyes. You hear the sounds of the lake, it's gentle ripples. You hear the quiet, calming song of this lake, the birds chirping in the distance and the occasional chirp of a stick insect. As you take another sip, the coolness spreads through your body once more. And then, you quietly drift off, simply listening to the calming sounds of the lake.

Guided Sleep Meditation to Relieve Stress and Worry (40 Minutes)

Welcome to this guided meditation to help you deal with stress and worry. If you find your mind is busy with your current worries and stresses, and find yourself struggling to quiet your mind and sleep, this meditation will guide you away from these thoughts providing you with relief, so you can have a peaceful night's sleep.

Now, lets us prepare for this session. Make sure you are lying down in bed, in whatever position you find most comfortable. Whenever you are ready, gently close your eyes. Taking the time to appreciate the complete experience of doing so. Notice how calming simply shutting out the rest of the world, and turning your focus inward really is.

Simply be in this moment. Allow your mind to be quiet, with any trains of thought just come to a stop. Remain here, simply focusing on your body as it relaxes. Right from the very top of your head down to the tips of the toes. Expect complete relaxation to come to you.

Now in your mind visualize what relaxation looks like. It may just be the feeling of your muscles becoming warm, loose and unbound from any tension. Alternatively, it may look like a special time or place in your life. Simply allow your mind to explore what relaxation looks like to you, feel as this feeling takes over your mind. All you need to think of right now, is relaxation.

As your mind explores what relaxation truly looks like, feel your muscles in all of your body begin to relax. You may come across any areas of tension in your body. If so, try and register these feelings in your mind. Throughout this meditation, any tension will gradually be released, leaving more and more room for you to sink into complete relaxation.

Now, turn your attention to your breathing. Notice how it makes your body feel. Observe the gentle rise and fall of your stomach as you breathe in and out. Notice how your chest moves in synchronization as if in a calming partnership. Each breath you take, brings you closer to a calming sleep. With every exhale, imagine all tension from within you is gradually carried away. Bringing you closer to a completely comfortable sense of peace.

Relish the feeling as relaxation moves through your body. With every exhale, feel as your body becomes lighter as tension is lifted away. Put no pressure on yourself, as even if you get only a little sleep, just a few hours can help you feel more energized and awake once morning comes.

Whilst you lay down and relax along with this meditation, notice as you feel more and more refreshed. With every inhale, enjoy the sensations the fresh, energizing air brings you. This energy stored away, readying you for tomorrow. Each breath brings you closer to the refreshed, rejuvenated version of you tomorrow morning.

If you find yourself falling into sleep right now, don't fight it, allow it to come. This meditation still has the power to influence your mindset positively, even in sleep. Simply leave your body and mind in control.

As you find yourself awakening tomorrow morning, you will feel refreshed. You will feel alert and completely prepared for whatever your day throws at you. This meditation will help you find the restful, peaceful sleep that you need.

Throughout this meditation, we will be using the power of your imagination to visualize your feelings of stress and worry, making these thoughts much easier to break down and leave behind. Using positive mental images, and the power it provides, you will be able to free your mind. Freeing your mind from any negativity, opens it up to feelings of peace and tranquility, that will help you drift into a restful, relaxing sleep.

Remind yourself that this moment is just for you. A time with no disruptions. Any worries or thoughts about any stressful situations going on in your life are not welcome here. This time is for rest. Time for you, for your sleep, so your mind tomorrow can be full of clarity.

Notice as you slip deeper into relaxation now. How you find yourself sinking further and further into the softness of your bed. How you feel totally relaxed, and as if one with your surroundings. Now, it almost feels as if your floating on a warm, fluffy, white cloud, perfectly soothing every inch of your body.

Now, you feel light and almost weightless, as if you are simply carried by the wind while you float peacefully. Whilst you feel light and free, all your muscles feel warm and heavy. Notice as they sink deeper and deeper into the softness of your mattress. You feel completely supported.

Allow your bed to provide you with all the comfort and protection you need. Allow it to hold you safely in place, comfortable and supported by its warm, softness. You sink deeper and deeper into state of complete calm. Enjoy the freedom of this moment, as you escape your stressful emotions, even if this is just for a brief moment. Allow yourself to slowly move closer to a deep, rewarding sleep.

As each second passes and with each and every breath, feel yourself become more rested. As you sink deeper into this state of peace, you give your body the opportunity to restore any energy that's been depleted. Know that this time you have given yourself is highly productive for your health and wellbeing. This time spent before you fall asleep, ensures your state of mind for tomorrow is improved upon. When you wake up in the morning, this positive energy will still be swimming around your body.

In a moment, we will bring in the power of visualizing thoughts and feelings. For now, simply continue to embrace relaxation flow through you. Take a moment to scan your body, noticing how nearly all tension has been completely washed away, like a refreshing wave of water has carried it far away. Return your attention to your breathing now, continuing to absorb this relaxing energy from the air. This powerful air helping to gradually clear your mind with every breath.

Now, imagine you are stood in the middle of a mountain range. Flowers and trees grow from the cracks in the large grey rock. All that surrounds you is beautiful. Far in the distance, you hear the gentle murmur of the waves crashing into shore. As you breathe in, you get a slight hint of this sea air pass through your nostrils. This experience gentle and inviting.

You walk upwards until you reach the peak of one of the mountain. You are completely surrounded by the wonders of this mountain range, with every shape of rock, from large boulders to tiny pebbles. Now you look out into the distance, finally you can see the ocean and a tiny beach attempting to hold its ground against the sea's waves. You watch as the waves hit into the side of the beach, but they move so gently you can barely hear them. The sound barely reaches you sounding like a calm, gentle breeze.

Enjoy this moment, and simply admire the scenery. You reach into your pocket and take out a rock, its black and appears to be moving. Confused, you hold it out in the light, it shines but not invitingly so, rather menacingly. Then a moment of realization hits you, you know what this rock is. This rock is something that you have been worrying about today. Something that has been weighing you down.

You find yourself looking down at the ground, noticing a small gap between the rocks. This gap is the exact size and shape of the rock you find yourself holding. You bend down placing the rock into this gap, it fits like a key. Now as you stand and let go, you watch as the dark colours of your rock, slowly fade away. They fade so much until it blends completely into the rock face, as if these worries had never even existed.

Now you have done this, you feel relief. Returning this negativity back into nature, where it can be used only for good, lifts all of your worries of your shoulders. A sense of gentle peace washes over your body and mind and you simply enjoy this moment with the faint sound of waves on the beach.

You start to continue your journey, descending the mountain on a small path leading you to the beach below. The path seems unused, vegetation and trees beginning to take over. Overhead is a chorus of birds, filling the air with their peaceful song as if they are cheering you on, on your journey.

Now the path finally opens up revealing the beach. Although the waves are so much closer now, they are still gentle, the sound is just so much more vibrant. Much easier to hear their rhythm. You keep walking until you find yourself right along the water's edge. You allow the incoming waves to wash calmly over your feet. The waves energy feels soothing and comforting. You bend down, allowing your hands to feel the waters refreshing energy envelop them.

Now, as you look to one side, you see a small pile of rocks. These rocks are black and alive, seemingly unattractive, just like the one you left at the top of the mountain. The rocks represent any of your current stresses. Right now, you find comfort in the fact there is no place for them here. With this in mind you know exactly what you must do.

You pick up, the largest, ugliest rock. It feels heavy and you reflect on how unnecessary and tiring it must be to carry this rock in your mind at all times. You carry this stone towards the waves, allowing the water to gently wash over it. Almost immediately, you find this stone you hold in your hand starts to lose its colour, the waves washing its colour away. Gradually, you find the stone starts to shrink in size, until it starts to dissolve leaving nothing left in your hands. This stone completely washed away, far into the vast ocean.

Now this stone is gone, you feel a deep sense of relief. As if an actual weight has been lifted from your shoulders, you feel liberated. Eagerly, you pick up the next stone in the pile, repeating this process. Gently lowering it into the water allowing the powerful ocean to work its magic. This stone once again loses its colour before dissolving completely into the ocean. Enjoy this experience, feeling complete relief as your troubles melt away into the ocean.

A gentle breeze flutters through your clothes. This breeze is soothing, especially as the midday sun glares down at you. You pick up another stone, holding it in front of you. Now, as this gentle wind rolls by, it begins to erode the stone. The stone shrinks down to a small pebble before eroding further into only a few grains of sand, that remain in your palm. You tilt your hand, allowing these grains to fall onto the beach, never to be seen again.

You pick up another stone from the pile, deciding to do the same again. Why have you been holding on to so much heaviness in your mind for so long? You examine this large rock in front of you, appreciating the calmness in your body and mind as it slowly erodes in front of you, until no more. This rock now only remains as grains of sand that slide between your fingers, dropping down and joining the beach around you.

You look beside you once more and notice there are no rocks left. You are completely free from stressful and worrying thoughts, there is nothing holding you back. These thoughts no longer occupy any space or dark corners of your mind once more. So with that you sit down, on the warm glistening sand and simply look out to the ocean. You fully appreciate this moment, this secluded place and all it has given you.

Now, you let go, and lie back, placing your head onto the sand and gently closing your eyes. You breathe deeply, allowing the sea air fill your lungs. You listen to the breeze and the waves gently break into shore. You fully embrace the calm feeling of this place and the inner tranquility it has allowed you to create. This place is always here, waiting for you to return, whenever you wish. This calming place has been created from the power of your mind. This power can also be used to push away any thoughts of stress or worry allowing you to completely enjoy a relaxing, refreshing night's sleep.

Now as you slowly drift off into sleep, take a few more deep breaths. Enjoy the saltiness of the air as it passes through your nose. Fully embrace the beauty of your surroundings, as they continue to make you feel at peace. Allow yourself to drift deeper and deeper into a blissful sleep. Look forward to waking in the morning completely relaxed and rejuvenated.

www.ingramcontent.com/pod-product-compliance
Lightning Source LLC
Chambersburg PA
CBHW081506080526
44589CB00017B/2671